PRAISE FOR *The P(*

MW00427551

"*The Power of This Thing Called Life* brings the voice of a spiritual master to life once again. 20th-Century American philosopher Ernest Holmes left a huge imprint on the world in the field of spirituality. His wisdom was timeless, and·this revised version makes it fresh and relevant for a new generation. Use it as a study guide to happiness and success."

Dr. Chris Michaels
Author of The Power of You

"Students of the world, searching for something to make them whole and something to bring joy into their lives, will find answers in *The Power of This Thing Called Life*. Here, Ernest Holmes shares basic truths of the universe and of God that will resonate with the reader. Every sentence is filled with wisdom, insight, and ways to capture the love and happiness we all seek. We have all the tools, and we're shown how to use them. The power is within us. I was reminded throughout the book of the simple nature of the feelings, thoughts, and emotions that comprise all action and reaction, and the resulting consequences."

Antonia Albany
Author, Golden Grace: Embracing the Richness of Our Later Years

"Newt List publications bring new life to classic works of metaphysics by revitalizing the language for the modern reader. In addition, by making the texts gender neutral, these exciting ideas about the creative power of mind become accessible in a potent new way because the barrier of antiquated writing conventions has been dropped. *The Power of This Thing Called Life* is beautiful, inspiring, and wonderfully engaging to read. This new book in the tradition of Newt List's updated classics is a keeper and a must have for serious students of spirituality."

Dr. Edward Viljoen
Author, The Power of Meditation

"This book has a simple, yet powerful message: One does not need to make things happen; one's job is to make things welcome. *The Power of This Thing Called Life* will teach you how to make your good welcome."

Rev. David Bruner, DD
Senior Minister & Spiritual Director

THE POWER OF
THIS THING CALLED LIFE

THE POWER OF
THIS THING
CALLED LIFE

ERNEST HOLMES

newt
LIST
Chicago • New York

Newt List
www.NewtList.com

ISBN-13: 978-0692116142 (Newt List)
ISBN-10: 0692116141

Printed in the United States of America

Published April 2018

Design by Randall Friesen

CONTENTS

CONTENTS

FOREWORD

Thirty years ago I walked into a church housed in a suburban shopping center. I don't remember much of what the minister said, but I do remember hearing "Change your thinking, change your life." And changing my life was exactly what I desperately needed to do.

Nothing was working. My happily-ever-after marriage was a thing of the past. My rebound relationship was a disaster. I had three children, no job. I had no prospects. And I had no idea what to do about any of it.

"Change your thinking, change your life." Why not? I had nothing to lose.

After the service I wandered into the church bookstore. The enormity of titles was overwhelming. I opened a few books whose covers or titles seemed promising, but nothing seemed to speak to me or my needs. Then I picked up a narrow volume called *This Thing Called Life*, by Ernest Holmes. I opened it randomly and found these words: "You are now about to enter into the greatest experience of your life—a conscious use of the God Power that is within you." A bell went off in my head.

I took the little book to the counter, paid for it and placed it very carefully in my purse, already thinking that if I was about to enter into the greatest experience of my life, I should treat my guidebook with the respect it deserved. I had no idea how prophetic those thoughts would be.

That little book opened the door to a way of thinking about myself and my relationship to life in an entirely new way. Although the words had been written decades earlier, the message they conveyed was timeless. Holmes' words spoke to something within me that longed for a greater understanding, and I responded with enthusiasm. I was developing a new dedication to living life at a higher level.

I returned to that church, to that bookstore, and to Holmes' writing again and again. Everything in my life became new, fresh, and exciting. His words shifted my perspective, revealed a new way of looking at my life, and pointed me in a direction that my soul urged me to follow. As I read about the possibilities for healing, for prosperity, for love, for success, I was first intrigued, then hopeful, then I began to put the ideas to use and become actively involved in my relationship with life.

As my thoughts began to change, my life began to change, and not only could I feel it, I could see it. Others noticed the change. For the first time ever I was directing my own creative transformation instead of being at the effect of accidental circumstance. It felt good.

Ultimately my life took a direction I could never, would never, have predicted. One morning I found myself sitting in that same church, listening, and thinking, "I wouldn't have said that *that* way. I would have said…" About the third time the thought occurred to me, a voice within me asked, "What are you going to do about it?"

My mind had changed. My life had changed. What I did was apply to, attend, and graduate from ministerial school. What I did after that was accept a position at a church where I put the teachings into action and created a twenty-year ministry teaching and sharing the ideas I found in a little book.

I have shared these ideas in countless talks. I have taught these lessons to hundreds of students. I love sharing these truths with others, I love watching lives change for the better, and I never stop benefiting from them myself. Holmes' words always speak to me, the lessons continue to teach me, and the truth I find in them never fails to reveal to me the miracles in This Thing Called Life.

Holmes' ideas helped me change my mind about who I was, what I was, and what I could be. They taught me about life and my powerful relationship to it. The words taught me that I didn't have to be a victim or a martyr, or settle for what was handed to me. I believed I was something much more than all of that, and that thinking changed my life.

In the decades since that fortuitous day in the bookstore, I have read and reread most of Holmes' books and I have been privileged to hear his voice on recordings of his radio show, which was also titled "This Thing Called Life." Holmes opened every show with the words: "There is a power for good in the universe, greater than you are, and you can use it." What followed was always a recipe for doing just that.

In addition to teaching the powerful truths that he called "The Science of Mind," the radio shows revealed something that his books could not. His presence was dynamic. His enthusiasm was contagious.

This book, *The Power of This Thing Called Life*, is a compilation of recordings of Holmes' radio show, and it is a jewel. The words and ideas remain true to their original writer, but the language has been lovingly and respectfully updated to include gender-neutral terms, and, through those judicious changes, the truth flows. It is as though you can hear Holmes speaking directly to you in a language of today about truths that are eternal and ageless.

Whether you are an old friend of the writer or a newcomer to these thoughts, you will find the ideas here will uplift and empower you. You will find truths that will alter your thinking, change your mind, change your life, and set you on the higher road to living the life of your dreams.

No matter where you find yourself in this moment, I am excited for you, because you are about to enter into the greatest experience of your life.

Rev. Dr. Marlene Morris

God Is Your Adventure

We are all in search of something that will make life worthwhile. And this something that we are in search after is God, the living Spirit, God the eternal presence, not a God that is far away from us but a God who is closer to us than our very breath. The discovery of God in yourself is the greatest discovery you can ever make.

You and I and everyone seem to be searching for something, as though we knew by some divine instinct within us that there is something that could really make us whole and happy, something that will include our physical well being and give us real success in living.

If we were to ask ourselves, "Just what is it I want from life?" I think our answer would be: We want friends; we would like to have people like us and we wish to like others; we want to enter into the joy of living; and, above everything else, we wish to be happy. We want to eliminate all fear from life and have an inward sense of security that makes us feel that all is well with us, not only in this world but in another world to come.

It has been my privilege over many years to discuss these thoughts with thousands of people, and I know that everyone's search is for God, because everyone is searching for something that will make them whole. Just as self-preservation is the first law of nature, everyone, whether or not they know it, is in search of the assurance that they will live forever somewhere. But everyone doesn't know or quite realize that they are really searching after God. This is because we have separated religion from everyday life. We have tried to separate life from living and God from nature. So, in some vague sort of way, we have come to feel that the realm of God is not really at hand, but rather that it is to transpire in a dim and unknown future.

This was not the attitude Jesus took when he proclaimed that the realm really is at hand; when he told us that if we would find God in ourselves and in each other and in nature, we should find happiness and completion; that we should find what the human heart not only longs for but absolutely needs, particularly in these times of stress and strain when the question arises from countless thousands, "What is it all about? Why this confusion and uncertainty and fear and doubt? Is there anything that can make us whole?"

I believe that out of this great confusion will come an equally great certainty, and out of all this doubt will grow a faith. It surely will if enough people turn to that divine source from which everything springs. God really is our adventure, and divine power alone can save the world from destruction.

As never before in human history, we need God. We need to enter into a close communion with the living Spirit and feel the warm embrace of its eternal presence around us. We need to know that we are not pawns on a checkerboard of chance, that there is a real and deep meaning to existence, a meaning that includes this life and everything in it, and, after this, a life to which we may look forward with happy anticipation. Nothing less than this can give us happiness and peace.

Perhaps at first thought it may seem a selfish desire to say we want this and we want that and we want something else. And yet it is impossible for us to think of anything as being entirely separate from ourselves. We cannot think of life without thinking of its connection with the self or its relationship to the self. We cannot think of others without thinking of their relationship to us.

The singer wishes to sing. The dancer wishes to dance. The business person wishes to be a success. The parent wants to provide for the family. Self-expression is not selfishness. Selfishness is seeking our individual good at the expense of others. Self-expression means that we live with others in happiness, giving to each the privilege of expressing every talent they possess and rejoicing with them in their success.

There is nothing wrong with self-expression. This Thing Called Life has entered into each of us in an individual way, animating everything we do and always urging us toward greater things, as though there were no limit to the expansion of the individual life. But we are so constituted that the greatest self-expression includes our relationship with others and our relationship with everything in life.

"This Thing Called Life" means God, and God means that invisible presence in the universe, that divine power which animates everything, that law of good which controls everything. Solomon, who was supposed to be one of the wisest people who ever lived, said, "With all your getting, get understanding." And Jesus, the most compassionate of all people, said "I have come that they might have life and that they might have it more abundantly." He said, "I desire that my joy shall enter into you; that the peace which I have shall be your peace and that the certainty that is mine shall be to each of you as an enveloping blanket of security, a feeling that all is well with you here and hereafter," because "it is your Creator's good pleasure to give you the realm."

Jesus also told us that if we find God, we will find all these things, because all these things are added to the great discovery. Jesus made heaven and earth come together. He did not say there is a heaven that

God has provided for you in a life after this life. He said that heaven is present with you. He said to the one who died with him, "Today you shall be with me in paradise." Jesus said that the realm of God is at hand, and he told us that everyone who comes into this realm through finding a right relationship with God will find love and friendship, success and happiness, here and now. Jesus never condemned the personal desire we all have to live happily and successfully.

The search for God is not the search for some abstract principle or some future state of being. Our search is to find that "something" right where we are, to discover that "something" in each other and in nature. The Psalmist said that the earth is filled with the glory of God, and we all know that the great teaching of Mahatma Gandhi was not that we should renounce the world, but that we should find God in the world. It is this finding of God, or This Thing Called Life, in everything we do and in every person and every thing we contact that is our real search.

The amazing and interesting thing we discover when we read history is that the great examples of the human race have been those who have found this something—something greater than they are and yet something that seems to be a part of what they are, something that stands big and tall in people, something that can give us the assurance that all is well, that behind the fear and doubt and uncertainty of life, there is a great assurance that at the center of the storm there is a place of peace, and at the center of every person we can find God.

The pathway back to human freedom and happiness will have to include the idea that God is not separate from God's creation but is part of it. God is our adventure, and the search is both an individual and a collective one. But as always, we must start with the individual, and that individual means you and it means me.

If our search for God happily results in our finding God, everyone around us will soon discover this fact. If our search for happiness makes us happy without robbing others, everyone we contact will be exposed to this happiness. It will become contagious. If our search is for love, we will find it. We will become lovable, and those around us will love us because we have first loved them. If our search for security finally leads us to the place where we are no longer afraid, everyone who contacts us will be lifted up because of our faith. They will be strengthened because of our strength, and they will feel secure in our security.

Have you and I actually and persistently tried to find God in each other? I'm afraid we haven't. There is no use blaming ourselves. It does one no good to beat their breast and exclaim how unworthy they are. This will merely add more confusion to an already disturbed mind. Searchers for God must learn to forgive themselves and everyone else, to forget even their own weaknesses as they seek strength. Searchers for peace must forget their confusion and meditate on peace, and, as they do this, they discover that the confusion disappears. Searchers of God may be sure of this. They will have to find God in themselves before they can discover God in others. This is why Jesus said that the blind cannot lead the blind; there must be a seeing eye.

When one of the disciples of John the Baptist came to him and exclaimed, "What shall I do to avoid the wrath to come?" John answered something after this manner: "My friend, I have not come to tell you how to avoid some future wrath that is to be visited on you. I have come proclaiming that the realm of God is already at hand." And this is the attitude we should take: that life holds nothing against us. It desires only our good. It wants us to be well, happy, and successful, but it wants us to play the game of life the way it is supposed to be played—in unity and cooperation with others.

These are the only rules that life has laid down for us. It hasn't demanded that we do something that is impossible. It hasn't told us that we have to understand something that only a few great intellects can comprehend. It hasn't even told us that we all have to become saints before we can enter into the realm of heaven. It has merely said this: Here I am. Accept me. I am truth. I am wisdom. I am love. I am peace, and I am eternal goodness.

A child can understand this, and this is why Jesus so beautifully exclaimed, "Suffer the little ones to come unto me, and forbid them not, for of such is the realm of God."

Suppose, then, you and I start all over, beginning right now, and let's see if we can't learn to forget all the heartache and sorrow and pain, all the fear, frustration, and uncertainty, and go back inside ourselves until we find that little child who isn't afraid, because, by some divine instinct within, it knows that "underneath are the everlasting arms."

Are we afraid of becoming that spontaneous child again lest someone think we are foolish? Well, who is there among us who wouldn't again be happy as a child? Who is there among us who would not recapture the dream of youth? We are "tired of building and spoiling and spoiling and building again, and we long for the dear old river where we idled our youth away; for a dreamer lives forever, but a toiler does in a day."

If the greatest person who ever lived has told us that we must become as little children, we need not be afraid of becoming childlike. Remember, childlike does not imply being childish or silly or foolish. Rather, it implies that sublime attitude scientists must have as they stand in awe before the majesty and might of the laws of nature. It is that childlike quality that the greatest mathematicians must have as they contemplate the infinity of numbers. It is that reaching out toward the essence of beauty that every great artist feels when they capture the glory of a sunset or the soft, radiant pathway of the moon across the water. We need not be afraid of being childlike. Rather, we should fear *not* to be childlike, because only through an attitude of faith and trust in the universe can we ever hope to recapture our lost paradise.

Your search and mine is for God, the great reality, the divine good that alone can give us a sense of security, the infinite and all-enveloping love that alone can give us the confidence to live. So let's try to find God in ourselves and in each other, and let's not be afraid to look for God in human events. And just as surely as we do this, we will find God. "Ask, and you shall receive; seek, and you shall find; knock, and it shall be opened unto you."

HOW THE
MIND OF GOD WORKS

There exist secret powers hidden within each one of us, powers that are transcendent of our ordinary faculties. We are so used to thinking that we are made up of flesh and blood and bone and hair that we lose sight of the more subtle powers of the mind. Yet, throughout the ages there have been people who have had transcendent powers that go beyond the bounds of physical laws as we understand them.

History is full of such records, and we have passed them over as being unusual and have lost sight of the simple fact that everything is governed by law. It is only in recent years that we have discovered the relationship between the mind and body. At first, it seemed impossible to believe that worry could produce a stomach ulcer or that people who are very sensitive might have considerable trouble with their throats, or that one who is in continual mental and emotional confusion is more subject to an ordinary cold than one who is calm and peaceful.

Today it is part of the ordinary procedure of a physician to inquire into the emotional reactions of the patient. It works something like this: If you would go to your physician today and say, "I am suffering with insomnia and break out with perspiration in the night and can't seem to get any rest," the doctor probably would inquire how you are thinking and try to discover the nature of your inner conflicts. The physician knows better than you do that a sleeping tablet is no permanent answer to insomnia. So the physician tries to find out the real reason for your restlessness, which is often some form of inner conflict, as though the mind were trying to go in two directions at once and, in so doing, keeps itself in such a turmoil that it finds no repose even in slumber.

Today, instead of speaking of a healthy mind in a healthy body, we say that there must be a healthy mind *before* there can be a healthy body. This is one of the great contributions that modern science has made to the field of medicine.

But it is more difficult to understand that our mental attitudes have such a direct relationship to other things. Today we speak of people who are accident prone, those who are more liable to have accidents than others, and important discoveries have been made along this line. It is now believed that eighty-five percent of our accidents are unconsciously invited.

In light of these facts, I would like to suggest some other ideas that I believe are equally as important. Investigations now being carried on in quite a number of our leading universities, in their psychological laboratories, are gradually bringing conclusive evidence that the mind reaches out into the future and can, under certain circumstances, foretell what is going to happen, just as it can reach back into the past and remember what already has happened.

The very latest discoveries, particularly at Duke University, under the able leadership of Dr. Rhine, are gradually collecting a lot of material that leads us to suppose that the mind is not confined to the body at all, but, in many respects, is completely independent of it.

I have no doubt that these new discoveries will gradually lead us to a complete acceptance of mortality. And I think it is wonderful that this investigation is being carried on independently of any of our dogmatic beliefs. These investigations are being conducted in a scientific manner, and the evidence that is gradually piling up will someday completely change our whole outlook on life.

I believe that we will come to understand that we are immortal right now. I believe it will show us that all people are immortal, not just some, and this is exactly as it ought to be, because we cannot believe that This Thing Called Life, which is God, has intended that some of us should be favored beyond others. Heaven has no favorites.

I believe it will be shown with equal certainty that our success or failure in life—whether we are happy or unhappy, prosperous or impoverished—is largely due to our mental attitudes, our faith and our fear.

There is another thing that seems equally true to me. All of us have a direct inlet, somewhere in our mind, to the mind of God. If so, then why shouldn't we become an outlet for the mind of God? Why shouldn't the mind of God flow through us and through our actions? Why shouldn't divine power animate everything we do? Why shouldn't the Spirit, which is present everywhere, protect and guide and counsel and direct us? This has been the hope of the ages, to find something bigger than we are, something that we can rely on with absolute certainty, something that is present with us here and now.

If it has been proven that the mind can look both forward and backward, it has with equal certainty been demonstrated that eternity is God's minute of time, and God's minute of time is the time you and I are living right now. It stretches backward and forward, but it is also present with us. We live in an eternal hour from which we may gather as much experience, as much good or as much evil, as we put into it.

We think of Jesus as the greatest person who ever lived. Yet it was

Jesus who told us that what he was doing, we should be able to do also, and he even added, "Greater things than these shall you do." Jesus plainly taught that every person is an inlet to the mind and the spirit and the power of God. He also taught that since we are inlets to this divine power, we may, if we will, become outlets for it.

The last fifty years of research into the hidden powers of the mind and spirit have given us evidence that everyone has a transcendent power of mind. But what is this elusive thing we call our mind? I believe the answer to this question is so simple that we have over-looked it. It seems to me that God, the living Spirit, can be thought of as a universal mind flowing through everything and a divine power animating everything and an infinite energy energizing everything. The mind of God, as a divine presence, is so close to us that it really is our mind. I believe there is one mind; that mind is God; that mind is my mind now. There is one life; that life is God; that life is my life now. There is one peace and poise and power that belongs to each of us, now.

Let's take this simple thought, then: "There is one mind; that mind is God; that mind is my mind now." Believing this to be true, let's see just how we are using this mind. In the first place, are we denying it or are we accepting it?

More than anything else, Jesus emphasized the thought that God is all there is. More than anyone else, Jesus proved his claim. He reached out and touched God in things and in people. As he did this, the miracle of life took place. The sick were healed, the multitude was fed, and innumerable other signs and wonders followed.

Naturally, everyone thought this person possessed a power that other people do not have. Somehow or other, we all seem to have overlooked the fact that Jesus actually told us that he didn't have a power that was withheld from others. He told us that he was using a power that we all have. Since Jesus was the one who made his claim good, he is the one for us to follow. I have no doubt but that our own well being and the salvation of the world as never before depends on an ever-increasing number of people trying to find out what Jesus was talking about, coming to believe in his claims, and learning to practice the few simple thoughts he gave us.

Jesus spent much time alone with himself and with God, on the desert and in the mountains or in the secret chamber of his own thought. How many of us are really practicing the presence of God? How many of us have learned to leave our confusion long enough to enter into a state of peace of mind? How many of us have laid all our fears and doubts and uncertainties aside long enough to draw assurance and faith and confidence into our being through communing with the divine Spirit, which really isn't outside us at all, only in the sense that it is present everywhere?

But really, the place you and I contact the mind of God must be at the center of our being, because here is the inlet, and we must learn to draw in before we can hope to give out. We must get back to the Spirit and increase our inlet if we expect divine power to flow through us and become an outlet to everything we do and say and think.

Nothing can hinder us but ourselves. You and I can have faith if we decide to have it. We can be lovable and kind if we wish to. We can turn away from fear and doubt if we will to. But, of course, before we can do this we must believe that we are working with an absolute certainty.

I cannot give you a reason to believe, and you could not give one to me. No one can give it to us. The reason why no one can give it to us is simplicity itself: How can someone else give us what we already have? The gift of life was made before we were ever born into this world. It came with us and it has been waiting through all our years of doubt, waiting on our acceptance.

This is why Jesus so often asked people, "Do you believe that I can heal you?" and so often said, "Your faith can make you whole." The mind cannot be filled with faith when it is full of doubt. It cannot be at peace when it is confused.

Let us take this thing out of the realm of mere theory or some beautiful sentiment that sounds good but produces no results. We want to know with certainty that there is a place—the Bible calls this "the secret place of the Most High"—within each of us, where we may and will dwell under the shadow of the Almighty.

At first, we might wish that someone else could do this for us, but it is fortunate indeed that this is impossible. If someone else had to do it for us, then we would not be whole and we could never hope to become whole. No one can live by proxy.

Let us then daily take time to practice believing that we are an inlet to the mind of God; believing that there is a love that, coming direct from the heart of the universe itself, can flow out from us in every direction, blessing everything it touches; believing that there is a certainty that can overcome every confusion and a faith that can destroy all fear.

When it comes to actual practice, we must remember that thoughts are things and that we actually give direction to a power greater than we are. We must understand that this power operates through, in, and upon our words, our prayers, and our affirmative meditations, and, in so doing, acts as a law of good. It is something you can depend on with complete certainty.

If, then, we are confronted with confusion, let's get quiet within ourselves and say, "God is not confused, so why should I be?" Let's say, "I believe there is an infinite peace flowing through me, and I am letting this peace flow out into everything I do. Moreover, I am stating definitely to every confusion in my own mind, or all the confusion around me, 'Be still, and know I am God'." And let's know that when we say, "Be still, and know," something is going to happen, something definite and positive and sure, because it will if we let it.

When we don't know just what to do or are uncertain how we should act, let's say, "But the mind of God in me *does* know what to do. It not only knows what to do, it is flowing through me now, telling me what I ought to do, and it is not only telling me what I ought to do, it is telling me to do it. There is an intelligence greater than I am that not only can but now *is* directing my path, and I am letting it."

When you say to yourself, "Something within me knows what to do and impels me to do it," you can turn any thought around and say, "Now you get out of here. You don't belong here at all. Just run away and mind your own business. I will have nothing to do with you." If you do this, you will discover that your affirmative thoughts rub out or erase the negative ones. They simply aren't there anymore.

Just keep right on making your affirmative statements, feeling that your mind is an inlet to God and knowing that, because this mind is positive and sure, something definite will happen.

Just do it! Gradually, a certainty will come to you, an assurance, and with it you will see signs following your own belief. They will be definite and positive. You will see conditions change with the change of your belief. The time will surely come when you will no longer flounder around in doubt or despair, because you will have learned the great secret of secrets, the secret of life itself—you are one with God now.

THANKSGIVING

If you love dogs and children, you have studied their reactions to the people around them and seen how important a little praise can be. You may say, "This is certainly true of children. They do love to be praised. They love to feel that they are important in the family life. But *dogs?*" Dogs also have a language of their own. When you talk to them, tell them how wonderful they are and look deep into their eyes, their tails wag and they kind of smile back at you as they lick your hand.

Dogs and children are not so far apart. Dogs and children know if you inwardly disapprove of them, whether or not you say anything. They reach out with a feeling toward you, and if that feeling is rebuffed, they are unhappy.

We all are children, just children of a larger growth and a little more experience, just children wanting to be loved, wanting to sing our little song and dance our little dance. We all like to strut our stuff and play the game of life with joy.

And we want to be adults. We don't want to appear too foolish. There is such a thing as the game of life, and there must be a way to play it so that when we go to bed at night, we won't carry too much of the hurt of the day into a restless sleep, and so that when we wake in the morning, we will anticipate something that promises to be wonderful and exhilarating.

This is the way we are made, and God never makes mistakes. There is nothing wrong with This Thing Called Life, because whatever seems wrong with it is the way we are living it. There is nothing wrong with life itself. If we are not getting the most out of life, it must be because we are not putting the most into it.

Thanksgiving means that we should be grateful for life, that we should praise the giver of all good, and that we should gratefully acknowledge the priceless heritage of being free and noble people.

How much time do we spend in affirming the good things of life, in recognizing that which is best in ourselves and others? In the exaltation of Spirit, the Psalmist exclaimed, "Bless the Lord, O my soul, and all that is within me bless God's holy name."

Mrs. Luther Burbank told me that her husband used to talk to his plants and tell them exactly why he planted them. A friend of mine who trains dogs talks to animals just as surely as you and I talk with each other, and just so surely do they respond. There is a principle here. If plants and animals and children respond to praise, why wouldn't everything else?

We want to find something in people and situations that will respond to us with joy and vitality. Suppose it is there all the time and our lack of acknowledgement merely obscures it? We would have to start with the simple proposition that there is something good at the center of everything, and that everything would be all right with our world if we could approach it in the right way, if we could meet people and situations in the right way, if we could get rid of all fear and sham and pretense, all of this false front we put up, and discover something real and genuine, something happy and whole at the center of everything.

There is a divine presence at the center of things that responds to us, and it ought to be so real that we feel it everywhere, in everyone and in every situation. Our starting point is to believe this not as a theory or an idle dream, but as something to be recognized and entered into here and now.

Jesus recognized God as the supreme presence in the universe, not only outside us, but within. He approached life and people as though this was true, and because he did, his life became a miracle. Everything he touched sprang into a newness of being. He didn't condemn the few loaves and fishes that the little child brought to him, but looked up to heaven and gave thanks for their increase.

Are you and I giving thanks and praising the increase? Are we gratefully acknowledging the good we wish to experience? Or are we condemning the little things in our lives so that they cannot multiply in our hands? After all, it is really the little things that count. Just as minutes run into hours and hours run into days and days into years and years fill up our lives, so it is that the little things that transpire from moment to moment really decide what our lives are to be and to become.

Recently I read of an experiment two people made with a couple of rose bushes. Each day, they blessed and praised one of the bushes, focussing on it alone, and in a few months the rose bush that was daily blessed responded with a lavish blossoming that far exceeded that of the other.

Suppose we apply this principle to everything we are doing—to people, to situations, and to our daily living—taking as our central thought that the divine presence is in everything and responds to us through everything. It is really a wonderful thing to thank God at every mealtime for the blessing of food. It is wonderful to bless each other for friendship. It will perform a miracle in your life if you consciously bless every situation you find yourself in.

Take time each day to say, "I bless every member of my family. I bless my spouse. I praise my children. I bless everything that they are doing." Bless the gifts you make to people. Bless the friends you have, and above everything else, don't forget to pray the prayer of blessing for the great and wonderful country that you live in. Bless your governmental leaders. Pray for everyone in places of public responsibility.

If you are in business, bless your business. Bless the customers that come in; bless the goods that go out. Bless everyone working with you or around you, and don't forget to bless your own effort, that it will prosper and multiply and increase and return to you hundredfold.

You are proceeding on the proposition that there is a divine presence in everything and everyone, and a divine law of good running through everything. Your recognition of this law, your acceptance of it, your prayer of affirmation about it causes this presence to respond to you in a new way. It rises to meet your expectation, your faith, your conviction, and your acceptance.

In doing this, don't pay too much attention to negative situations. Try to bring a positive affirmation to bear on everything that is negative. You will soon find that the negative things will tend to disappear and the positive will take their place. This will have a very interesting effect on you personally. You will find a new lightness coming into your step, a new sense of joy into your mind, and a growing, deep, and abiding conviction that God really is in heaven and that heaven is wherever you happen to be.

Here is one more thought I would like to add. Try to give thanks even for those things that you do not see. The Bible says, "Blessed are they who *not* having seen, still believe." In other words, when Jesus blessed the loaves and fish, he was blessing the increase that he knew God would provide, and his faith and expectancy reached out to the law of good in such a way that there was an immediate manifestation of more.

Jesus hadn't seen all the loaves and fish that were needed to feed the multitude, but he blessed this invisible substance. He gave thanks for this increase, and this you must do also. God never lets anyone down. Particularly, try to bless yourself. Bless your hopes, your aims, and your aspirations.

Bless the faith that is in you, and it will grow. It will bloom like the rose bush. Bless the unused talents that you possess, and new ways of doing things will come into your experience. There is no way that God can work for us other than by working *through* us, and if we reject the gift of life, if we refuse to accept it, how can we ever hope to hold it in our hands?

Be sure that you don't make a drudgery of this. Let it be a song of praise, a joy in blessing, a gladness in giving, just as spontaneous as was the faith of the little child who brought those few loaves and fish and placed them in the loving hands of Jesus.

Isn't it wonderful that out of all that vast throng of people who needed to be fed, the only person in that great congregation who really entered into the spirit of what Jesus was doing was a little child with the bread and the fish? Jesus and the little child were the only two people in that gathering who didn't know that it couldn't be done, and Jesus apparently wanted the cooperation of someone who did know that it could be done, just as he knew.

I love to think of that little child, eyes bright with enthusiasm, little toes into the dirt, and the hand of expectancy outstretched, willing and glad to surrender a morsel and without the slightest question in mind about the increase.

Let's you and I see if we cannot become as little children. It is natural for us to believe. It is natural for us to dance with joy and enter into the rhythm of life with happiness, and it is natural for us to expect the miracle of love to perform its act of kindness.

We are either talking about the greatest thing in life or we are following a forlorn hope that could lead only to despair. We may be certain that we are talking about the greatest thing in life. There is an inner presence that responds to us. There is a law of good that works for us. There is a power of right that can rearrange all of our circumstances, if we believe it can.

Suppose we try this week to discard our negative approaches to people and circumstances, and for every condemnation, let's find something to praise. For every doubt, let's find a faith. For every fear, let's have a new hope. Let's see if we can't sing our song of praise and thanksgiving. I know if we practice this for the next few days, a new flavor will come into our living, and when we gather around that festive board, we, too, will be able to say with the Psalmist, "Bless the Lord, O my soul, and all that is within me, bless God's holy name."

ENTHUSIASM: GOD'S MEDICINE

Every normal person wishes to be well, happy, and successful, and there is nothing wrong with this. Sometimes we think that perhaps life withholds these good things from us, as though it didn't wish us to enter into the joy of living. And yet, Jesus said, "I am come that they might have life, and that they might have it more abundantly."

It is this more abundant life that we all seek. The interesting thing about it is that we go in quest of it just as though we knew it were there, as though something had told us this before we were even born. We seem to feel and to know that life is made to be lived, because how could there be a song unless someone sings it?

You have often seen a group of children tramping off to a ball game or going swimming, always expecting to have fun. How their eyes sparkle and the corners of their mouths turn up! They are laughing, singing, dancing, following some natural rhythm, as though joy were at the center of everything.

There is an abandonment in them, a carefree attitude, and so often we say, "Isn't it too bad they must grow up and become disillusioned, that they have to enter the struggle for life and gradually be worn down with it until the child in them is dead?" With the poet, we think, "Turn backward, turn backward, O time in thy flight, and make me a child again, just for tonight."

But somehow or other, we feel this is all wrong. We do not feel and we cannot believe that This Thing Called Life meant it this way. We know, as though something were always telling us that we are created to be glad, to rejoice. What happened to us, when we became adults, that dampened this spontaneous joy and robbed us of that zestful anticipation that gives skill to the hands and speed to the feet?

It is a lack of enthusiasm. It is a lack of being able to enter into the game of life and play it, not merely as an onlooker but as a participant, because we want to be out there pitching, too. We want to be out there batting for a home run.

My mother lived to be nearly one hundred years old merely because she had an enthusiasm for life. Right to the last moment it was that way. There was nothing heavy or weighty about it, nothing sad, not even a sigh, no regrets, just a passing on from the twilight of this day into the dawn of a new tomorrow.

This is the secret: entering into the Spirit of life, into the joy of living, into the usefulness of being alive. No one can grow old if they have faith and enthusiasm. We need to rediscover the well-springs of the childlike joy that gave us the happiness, the security, and the faith we had as children.

We learned to be afraid. We learned to be unhappy. We learned to be depressed. There is nothing wrong with This Thing Called Life. God cannot make mistakes. Our inner conflicts and all those emotional states that make us unhappy and depressed are a direct result of our having blocked the natural, normal, and spontaneous joy of life.

It is this joy of living that we wish to recapture. Only those who still possess this priceless gift when they become adults can stay young and happy. Every possession on earth, all the honors that can be bestowed on us, everything that the world has to offer cannot compensate for the lack of enthusiastic and spontaneous joy.

The reward of growing up is seldom worth the price the child in us pays for it. But of course we have to grow up; we must become adults. But why couldn't this be done without surrendering everything within us that is childlike and natural and spontaneous?

Let's re-examine children and see what they have that we have forgotten about. In the first place, they have no fear. They aren't morbid. They aren't unhappy. They have an enthusiastic zest for living. They expect to get a kick out of life. They expect their parents to provide for them. They don't even wonder whether or not their food is going to digest. They aren't bothered with insomnia. They don't have stomach ulcers. They just live and sing and dance and are glad. They don't even know that they are bad until some unwise person tells them.

If we are going to recapture this lost dream of youth, we will have to return to the same place of confidence in life that we had when we were children. We must have the same confidence in something greater than we are that children have in their parents. The family life is Earth's symbol of the realm of God. Here is security, peace, comfort. Here is a sense of belonging, a spontaneous and enthusiastic joy in living.

One of our greatest needs is that we find an emotional relationship to This Thing Called Life, to God the living Spirit, to that power greater than we are; that we find the same kind of relationship, but broadened and deepened, that we had for our human parents. Jesus understood this better than we do. This is why he said that the realm of heaven is like a child. "Suffer the little children to come unto me, and forbid them not, for of such is the realm of heaven."

Jesus was an adult when he said this. He was mature in thought, but he had not lost the great secret of life. He had not forgotten that "celestial palace" from which he came. He knew that he was one with God and one in God. He had already discovered that the loving protection of the human home—the greatest institution on Earth—was only a symbol of another protection in another family, the protection of the living Spirit and the family of the whole human race.

Jesus knew that you are some part of the whole scheme of things. He said that your Creator knows what you have need of; that if you ask God for bread, you won't receive a stone; if you ask for joy, you will not receive grief; if you ask for life, you will not receive death. As the child in him grew into the greatest person of the ages, he never lost that enthusiastic approach to life and trust in God.

It is now known that a lack of enthusiasm causes most of our physical weariness, that the sense of insecurity, worry, and anxiety which attends this produces many of our physical troubles. Joy and enthusiasm are as necessary to our physical well being as is the food we eat.

So our problem is simplified. We wish to remain children in the larger family, children of a universal parentage. We want to have the same feeling that we had when we were children, yet still be responsible adults. This cannot be done without confidence in life. There is nothing—no mental attitude, no emotional reaction, no intellectual conception—that can in the slightest degree take the place of the sublime trust that the child has.

Perhaps by now you are saying, "Are you telling me that I have to become religious?" Exactly that, no more and no less. But of course I don't mean that you must believe the way I do. Everyone will have to figure this out for themselves.

Common sense will tell you that just as the tree must be rooted in the soil from which it draws its sustenance while lifting up its branches to the sun and the light and the air of heaven, so you and I will have to feel ourselves rooted in something from which we draw our life. After all, what does religion mean other than our relationship to this invisible thing we call life? What is a prayer other than communion with the divine presence that exists everywhere?

Science has unlocked many a secret of nature and even exposed the energy hidden at the center of the atom. Then why is it that today so many of our leading scientists are counseling that we get back to God? In the last few decades, psychology has uncovered many secrets of the human mind, those hidden and almost unknown causes of so much of our distress. Why is it that today so many of our leading psychologists are counseling a return to the life of faith?

We may study all the philosophies of the human race since time began, and such comfort as we glean from them will not be the comfort of intellectual gymnastics but that comes only from those passages, from Socrates and Plato to Emerson, that tell us that "the finite alone has wrought and suffered, and the infinite lies stretched in smiling repose."

It is one of the most helpful signs of our times, that in the midst of all this confusion, doubt, and fear, there is a reaching out—or in or back to—This Thing called Life. I am content to call it religion, because I know that the world can no more exist without religion and remain happy than the physical body can exist without food and remain healthy. This is the way we are made, and all the wit of human beings cannot change one bit of it.

No, I am not trying to convert you to any particular kind of religion—most certainly not mine. I am talking about the essence of all religions, because the essence is identical. It is a belief in God, and an enthusiastic belief, not just an intellectual one.

Enthusiasm reaches out with joy; there is nothing depressing about it. It reaches out in faith; there is no fear in it. It reaches out with acceptance; there is no doubt in it. And it reaches out as a child;

there is no uncertainty about it. Just a joyful trust in life, just a happy outlook on living, just a complete assurance that we can have confidence in God.

Let us awaken the joy in us again and enter into the game of living, not sitting on the sidelines, but out there in the field, pitching.

LOVE:
THE LODESTONE OF LIFE

Humankind's three greatest needs are: to feel that we are needed, wanted, and loved; to feel that we belong to the universe in which we live; and to have an object, or objects, on which to lavish our affection. It is now known that most unhappiness comes from a sense of being rejected, of not being wanted, needed, and loved. It is also known that a large percent of our physical troubles is a direct result of emotional congestions that follow in the wake of feeling that we don't belong to life.

We call these things repressions, inner conflicts, frustrations, and sometimes we call them inferiority or superiority complexes. All these terms really refer back to our three fundamental propositions. We are so constituted by This Thing Called Life that we want to love and be loved, we want to sing and dance and be glad. We want to be a friend and have friends.

You can't beat nature at its own game. At least, no one has ever yet succeeded in doing so. We are born with an urge to express life. We are born with a desire to unite our living with others, to enjoy people and to live creatively. It seems as though something dynamic entered into us when we were born, an impulse to enter into the joy of living and to give vent to those thoughts and feelings, those emotional urges and impulses that every normal person has.

You might ask, "What has all this got to do with love?" It has everything in the world to do with love. Love is the givingness of the self, the imparting of the self to others, the projection of the self into the activities of life. Love is one of the supreme emotions in your life. Without love, everything is drab and without meaning.

But love has another need of its own. It must be loved in return. You not only wish to love others, you also wish them to love you. Otherwise, the circle isn't complete. When you love others and they return this affection, you are happy. But if your love is rejected, then you feel isolated and alone, unhappy and depressed.

A large percent of juvenile delinquency is the result of a lack of affection, cooperation, and understanding in the family life. Love really is the integrating factor of the family. Children must feel wanted and needed and loved. They must feel that they are understood and appreciated. They must feel the warmth and the color of affection.

If you were to trace the mental, emotional, and spiritual background of most criminals, you would probably find that they were conditioned early in life to feel a sense of rejection. Their emotional craving for affection had been rejected. Because of this, they feel isolated, separated, as though they were alone in the world. Therefore, they feel that they must build up an aggressiveness that fights everything down.

One of two things generally happens to children who feel rejected. They either retire within themselves and become anti-social, or, in self-defense, they build up an aggressiveness that is hard to govern. They are stubborn, obstinate, and willful. But if we were to examine more carefully, we might discover that they are merely building a wall around themselves.

We all have a need for each other. If you were to read the many hundreds of books on this subject that have been written in the last several years and boil them down to their real meaning, I believe this is what you would find: that you are born out of the creative urge of life to express itself, and when you entered this life, even as an infant, this urge was already there. You didn't put it there. It is an urge to live, to love, to create, to find happiness, to feel needed and loved, to cooperate with others and have them cooperate with you. When this doesn't happen, you feel frustrated and unhappy and alone.

It is said that when we are unhappy, there are four great adjustments that need to be made in our mental and emotional lives. The first adjustment is to the self, to try to find out who you are. What am I? Do I make sense? Am I worthwhile? Am I somebody in my own right?

The next adjustment is to those immediately around us, and, early in life, this means the family. What is my family's relationship to me? Am I a part of the family life? Am I wanted? Am I needed? Am I loved? Do I belong?

The third adjustment is to society, the world in which we live. Is life for me or against me? Are people trying to tear me down or build me up? Can I trust them? Can I believe in their sincerity? Do I dare to have affection for them? Do I dare express it? Do I feel that I will be rejected, laughed at, cast out?

The last adjustment is to life itself, to This Thing Called Life. Have I a personal and intimate relationship to it, or am I of no more account than "a feather wafted downward from an eagle in its flight"? Does the universe itself make sense? Is there a God? If so, does this God love me? Can I love this God? Do I feel at home in the universe? Can I have confidence? Can I have trust and faith? Is it safe for me to believe in God, in life, in people, in myself?

At least seventy-five percent of our chance to be physically well, mentally and emotionally happy, and to live a successful life depends on making these adjustments. So we are dealing with something very vital, something that is a personal problem to each one of us, and something we need to know about.

Let's start, then, with the first adjustment, which is to myself. Who am I? What am I? Why am I here? What will I do with myself? What is this strange emotion I feel that makes me want to like people and have them like me in return? Am I a part of something bigger than I am or am I alone, buffeted by fate?

There is only one answer to this. You belong to the universe in which you live. A power greater than you are has put you here. You can't fight it, you can't deny it, and you can't get away from it. God wanted you and needed you, otherwise you wouldn't be here.

You can trust this "something" you call life. It is not only where you are, it is *what* you are. It is in as well as around you, and its whole impulsion is love. The universe rests on the shoulders of love. Love is the lodestone of life. The very fact that when you were born, you reached out in trust to those around you is proof enough of this.

Just accept, then, that no matter what your experience may have been up until now, the truth about you is that even though you were born of human parentage, the thing that is really you, that came through this human parentage, is an original, creative, wonderful thing. You are God's beloved child. You don't have to make this up. It isn't just an idle sentiment. It isn't a platitude. It is real. It is the truth about you. Accept it and be glad.

The next proposition is that this is also true about everyone you will ever meet. Everyone has the same feeling that you have, the same desire and the same need, and no one can be happy until they have worked out a right relationship with This Thing Called Life—God.

Just make up your mind that you live and move and have your being in that which is the very Spirit of life itself, whose whole impulsion is love, whose whole desire is to give.

But perhaps God, like us, also needs that you return to God this affection that God has for you. If it is true in your human relationships that your desire for love and affection must be met by that which loves in return, don't you think that the greater life, which has given you this life, must have the same desire? Of course it must.

You must learn to have confidence in life, to believe it, to trust it, to have faith in it. You must come to feel that it returns that love and confidence, that as your love goes out to it, its love returns to you multiplied, just as it does when you love people, because love begets love, confidence inspires confidence, and faith is met with faith.

Having come to the conclusion that you belong to the universe, that even God has need of you, and that love is really the well-spring of your life, learn to feel this about all people. Behind the mask that people so often wear, the attitude of coldness they assume, there is always that soft, tender thing in the strongest person as well as the gentlest. Reach back to it. Unite with it.

This is your adjustment to life. This alone can make you happy. Don't feel that in doing this you will become a mere sentimentalist, that you will become weak or inefficient. Quite the reverse. It will make you self-reliant. It will give you confidence in life. It will help you to get along with people. It is a sure guide to the only success that is worthwhile.

Jesus said, "As I have loved you, love one another." I don't think we could call Jesus a weak character, this person who could perform miracles, the one who was able to resurrect himself and triumph over the grave, he whose power stilled the wind and the wave. Perhaps he was the only really normal person who ever lived. What do you think?

New Lives for Old

Would you like to trade in your old car for a new model without any extra expense to yourself? Would you like to refurnish your home? Wouldn't it be strange if your car or home could remodel themselves, so that nothing about them could wear out? This sounds kind of fantastic, doesn't it? Yet, we are told that none of us is more than a year old physically, that our entire body is renewed every year.

If we would inquire into the possibility of rejuvenation, perhaps This Thing Called Life has already provided the solution, giving us new bodies for old as we travel along the pathway of life. But what about the mind? It is now becoming accepted in some groups that the mind does not grow old, that the mind of a ninety-year-old is as young as a child of ten, that while maturity slows it down somewhat, at the same time there is no reason to believe that the mind really ages.

This seems a strange proposition, that we should not be over one year old physically and that the mind really doesn't age at all. Where, then, do the wrinkles come from, because most of us past a certain age have them. The answer doesn't seem to be in nature as much as in ourselves, because we certainly are using the same mind that we did years ago, and the body is being daily renewed. What is it, then, that grows old?

The Bible tells us to be transformed by the renewing of the mind and the putting off of the old person and putting on the new one, which is Christ. In another place, it says, "Behold, I make all things new." Perhaps this is another way of saying that God and the Spirit within us, which must be some part of God, cannot grow old. "I am the same, yesterday, today, and forever."

Why is it, then, if life itself is forever new and forever young, that we who live in it and from it experience age? The answer to this problem is not to be found in nature, which forever renews itself, nor in God, who is the creator of us all, but in ourselves. Always we are looking for the perennial fountain of youth outside the self. We go in search after the waters of life, not knowing that they are already gushing from the center of our own being.

Nature has provided for eternal youth. Spirit, which is life, is forever flowing through us, but we seem to be able to stop its progress. Just as we can tie a cord tightly around the arm and so inhibit the circulation of blood so that congestion, stagnation, and infection follow, in like manner we must have blocked the passage of This Thing Called Life through us.

Each time we enter a new year, it would be well for us to consider what we are carrying into the new year that doesn't belong. Have we really freed ourselves from the burdens and the cares of yesterday, or are we carrying them like dead things into tomorrow? Yesterday has forever passed, and tomorrow will forever elude us. Today is the only day in which we can really live. Isn't it wonderful that life has already provided for the day in which we live?

All God's plans are perfect, and at the time when we will have learned to follow the pathways of God, we will discover they are pathways of peace, joy, and happiness. Jesus said, "These things have I spoken unto you, that my joy might remain in you and that your joy might be full." When he left, he said that he was going to prepare a place for us that is better even than this. He plainly told us that we came from God, live in God, and return unto God. The whole life and teaching of Jesus was to show the relationship we have with This Thing Called Life, with the Spirit that is within us, around us, and through us, and with the divine intelligence that governs everything.

It is the habit of many to make great resolutions on New Year's Day, and it is a good thing to set an ideal before the mind. The Bible tells us that the most effective way to do this is to put off the old person and put on the new, which is Christ, and to be transformed by the renewing of the mind. "Christ in us, the hope of glory" means that the life of God has already entered into you, otherwise you would not be here. The mind of God is your mind, otherwise you could not think. Christ, or the child of God, is where you are and what you are, otherwise there wouldn't be any *you*. Nothing can be simpler than this.

How would it be if we were to start each new year with just one simple resolution: to try to live as though the realm of God were at hand, to try to believe that this physical body is being daily renewed and that the circumstances and situations in our lives are governed by a supreme intelligence that knows what to do and how to do it and is willing to do it?

Let's trade in the old physical body with all its weaknesses, its aches and pains, and see if we cannot transform it by the renewing of the mind, by thinking of the perfect life that exists at the center of every cell, every action, every function, every organ of the body.

Life and *God* mean the same thing, and if life is present everywhere, which it most certainly is, then God is present everywhere. It isn't as though we had to coerce life or argue with it or concentrate on it or will it into being, because we don't have to do this at all. What we should resolve to do is to feel, sense, imagine, and accept the flow of life through us.

Perhaps we will discover that it is the mind and not the body that needs to be renewed, that the transformation in both body and circumstances which we so greatly desire will be made possible only through first changing our thinking.

Let's begin, then, and trade in our old model of thought about the body for the one we wish to use during the next year of our lives. Let's keep our physical bodies one year young and not one year old. You may ask, "Just how am I going to do this?" The answer is simple enough. Every time you think of your body, think of it as your spiritual body. Think of every organ, action, and function of your physical body as being in pure and perfect Spirit. Think of God as being in you, around you, and through you. Think of every breath you inhale as the breath of life. Think of the food you eat as spiritual substance always nourishing the body. Think of the two coming together in perfect harmony.

Affirm perfect circulation, perfect assimilation, and perfect elimination. Declare that, in pure Spirit, there is no stagnation, no inaction, no over-action, no false action. God cannot make mistakes, and your spiritual body is a part of God's realm. There is a spiritual pattern at the center of every organ, every action, every function. If there were nothing to interfere with the passage of this spiritual pattern from the center of your being to the surface, all would be well. This is why the Bible says that the issues of life proceed from the heart, and "as we think in our heart, so we are."

Therefore, in trading in your model of last year's body, be sure that you get a good deal. Accept nothing less than the daily transformation of the body through the daily renewal of the mind. Thoughts really are things in a very true sense. Jesus said, "I am the light of the world" and "You are the light of the world." There is a light at the center of your being. It is a perfect light, put there by This Thing Called Life. Be sure this light shines in your new model, and since neither you nor I nor anyone else could have the power or the intelligence to put that light there, the only thing we can do is to stand aside and let the light that God put there shine for us.

You must be sure that the light of the new model shines brightly. You must be certain there is plenty of power to keep it going. You are going to need oil to keep it from squeaking and stopping. You are going to need faith and confidence, love and assurance. You are going to need to know that your power comes from the source of all power, which is God. And God is right where you are, and God is what you are now, not by and by. It is going to be interesting to see what happens to you when you do this. I am sure that in a few months you will be happily surprised.

Let's swap a few other old models now. How about unhappiness? How about fear? How about depression? How about loneliness? Let's take the old model to the factory of life and see what we can exchange it for. They have a lot of new models in there. When you get in the best one of all and go out on the highway, you discover that you are riding in a model that knows there is nothing to be afraid of. You are sitting in a model that loves everyone. It likes the country through which it is passing. It is not sensitive.

This is a good model, and you have made good deal. You didn't pay any difference. Or if you did, the whole price you paid was paid in the coin of thought, in the coin of attention and a careful training of your mind, in the coin of spiritual values that put their trust more in God than in anything else. You really were not anything out of pocket when you took in that old model and said, "It is no longer any good. Might as well throw it in the scrap heap or junk it." Think of the new one you got! Surely if nature has intelligence to renew this physical body every year, can't it renew your love, your friendship, and everything else in your life?

There is another deal you want to make. Trade in all your disappointments. Trade in all your losses and failures. Trade in your fear of lack and want. Trade them for that new model mentioned in the Bible, where it says, "Prove me now herewith, said the Lord, if I will not open you the windows of heaven, and pour you out a blessing, that there will not be room enough to receive it." Last, but not least, trade in all fear for faith. Faith is the only safe model in which to ride. Trade in hate for love. Love is the only safe driver to have at the wheel. Trade in all your doubts for certainty. Only certainty knows the road ahead.

Remember, God's factory is never shut down. There are no strikes, no lock-outs. There is no mismanagement. There is always plenty of material. The machinery never gets out of order. The assembly line is always running, and the deliveries are certain wherever you happen to be.

The power that sets the stars in their course knows all about you. The imagination that painted the sunset knows how to splash a little color in your pathway, and the immutable law that holds everything in place won't have the slightest trouble in taking care of you. Old lives for new, old bodies for new, old circumstances for new, old thoughts for new. "Behold, I make all thing new."

YOUR ALADDIN'S LAMP

If someone were to ask you, "Did you know that you are a genius?" would you laugh at this or would you take it seriously?

You may remember the story of Aladdin and the lamp. When Aladdin rubbed his lamp and made a wish, the genie would appear. Jesus said, "There is a light that lights everyone's path." He added, "If you put your light under a bushel, then no one can see it." It is this light that is the light of God and the light of life that is your light.

The question is not whether there is a genius hidden at the center of your life, but whether or not you are rubbing your lamp so the genie can appear. How could all the deep wishes, hopes, and aspirations of your life be there unless it was possible for them to be fulfilled? God never makes mistakes, and God put them there.

There is a power in the universe, and this power is available to everyone. It is the power that brought everything into being, therefore it is all power. It is not only all power, but it is all presence. It pervades everything, and it is at the very center of your own being.

If you wish to use this power, you must believe that it actually is there and make yourself an instrument for its action. Aladdin had to rub his lamp before the genie appeared, and Jesus tells us that we have to believe before it can be done unto us. This implies that you can actually think yourself into a mental position which makes it possible for the power to flow through you and out into the things you are doing. For instance, if you wish to be successful, rub your lamp with the idea in mind of success. See yourself as a success. Remove all fear and doubt, and you will have connected your desire with that power which is the cause of everything.

If you say to yourself, "There is one mind. That mind is God," you should also say, "That mind is my mind now. It is now guiding and directing me, causing me to know what to do and how to do it." This mind is your Aladdin's lamp, and the thoughts and ideas that come to you when you rub this lamp through faith and conviction are the genie that appears.

The great genius of Jesus lay in the fact that he was not afraid to trust God, and because he trusted God, he believed in himself. We can well imagine that it must have taken years of patient trying to come to the place where he dared to command the wind and the wave to be still, and yet, as you carefully study what Jesus did, how he thought, and what he said, you will be amazed at his simplicity and childlike acceptance.

For instance, he said that if you are praying for something, when you think about it (because, of course, you couldn't pray for it without thinking about it), try to accept in your own mind that it is already done unto you. It is this faith that is your Aladdin's lamp.

If Jesus had made this claim merely for himself and had said, "I am the only one who can do it," then there would be no hope for the rest of us. But Jesus actually said, "What I am doing, you can do also. You also have a light." He plainly taught that there is one life, one power, and one presence available to everyone.

It takes a little imagination for us to appreciate the meaning of this. Perhaps imagination really is Aladdin's lamp. But Aladdin believed that when he rubbed his lamp, something would appear. The genie would spring into being for him and do his bidding. Aladdin was a mythical figure, a character in a fairy story, and we read about him with keen delight because we feel we would like to be Aladdin. We wish we had a lamp that we could rub. We wish that there might be a genie who would appear at our command.

Aladdin was a mythical figure, appealing to our imagination, pleasing our fancy, delighting us with the thought of limitless possibilities. But Jesus, the way-shower, was not a mythological figure. He was a real person, and we cannot doubt that he was the greatest genius who ever lived. For a long time, we have thought of his teaching being so far away from our personal experience, so separated from the realities of life, as though he were talking about some future good, something impossible to attain here and now.

Although I had read the Bible more or less continually since I was a child, several years ago I got the idea that I would like to read the New Testament over again with this one thing in mind: to read the story of the life of Jesus just as though I were reading some other story, from the thought that such a person really lived, really said the things we read about, actually meant them, and did really prove his position in what he did. I became so interested that I spent all the time I could find for two years reading and thinking and trying to reinterpret everything Jesus said and did from this simple viewpoint.

Here was a person who knew what he was talking about. He knew it because he was able to do it. The thing that really amazed me was the simplicity of his teaching, the complete directness of it—his intimate relationship with God, his inward feeling of the divine presence as a living reality in and through everything, and his complete conviction that there was a law of good that responded to his faith. It was this utter simplicity that amazed me. I was so completely convinced all over again that I actually wrote a book about it, *The Philosophy of Jesus*. As a matter of fact, it was because of these two years devoted to this study that I happen to be talking to you today.

I am completely convinced that there is a power within you that you didn't put there, but that you can use—a power for good that is available to everyone and is available right where you are today. Jesus did not say it would come by and by. The one thing that made the deepest impression on me was that Jesus believed in the actual, active presence of God in everyone's life, and in no place did he ever infer that this power would not be available to you. Rather, he said, "I am telling you about a presence that is real. I am telling you how to use a power that actually exists and is really right where you are."

I am going to ask you to get out your lamp and rub it—rub it with faith and conviction, rub it with grateful acknowledgment and acceptance, rub it with feeling and imagination. You need have no fear for the outcome. Your mind is only a conductor for a power that actually is. Your light is borrowed from a universal light. The wick of your individual lamp runs deep in the oil of a universal life. It draws its power from a limitless source, because God is all the power there is, all the presence there is, and all the life there is.

Many of you will remember that when you were children, you used to trim oil lamps and polish the globes so that the light would shine brightly. Let's think of this other light in the same way. The wick must be trimmed, as Jesus said, keeping your light trimmed and burning. The globe must be clear and transparent so that the rays of light can shine out into what you are doing. But the light itself and the oil that furnishes its glow is something life has already done for you. What you are to do is to consciously hook up your mind with the person inside you—God's good person, God's perfect person.

Jesus said, "It is not I, but the Creator who dwells in me that does the work." Robert Louis Stevenson spoke of his "little mental brownies, who do half of my work for me even when I am asleep, and in all human likelihood do the rest for me as well when I am wide awake." When you go to sleep, you can turn all your ideas over to the genius within you. Rub your lamp of faith for a few moments and go to sleep knowing that the little genie will appear, and when you wake up in the morning, ideas will be there. Seize them with enthusiasm, and work on them with conviction.

Some people have called this "awakening the subconscious," and probably they are right. They say there is something inside you that, through imagination, can be stimulated into action, can work out all your problems even while you are asleep. I have known many inventors who said their ideas came that way. I have known lots of writers who do this. I have known mathematicians whose problems are worked out while they are asleep. The experience is so common that many books have been written on it. It has been called "the person inside you" and "the workshop of the unconscious." But you and I are not particularly interested in what anything is called. Rather, we are interested in what it is, how it works, and what it does.

Your whole mind, whether you call it conscious or subconscious, is merely an instrument of the Spirit within you. It is the place where this ever-present Spirit is focalized through you as a person, expressing itself in you as an individual. Technical terms will not help us any. I notice that, in the life of Jesus, he just called it *God within him*. It was his terrific simplicity that has eluded us, and now, gradually, we are working back to its meaning, to the discovery that everyone's life is hid with Christ in God, that there is a power and a presence at the center of your being that can be called forth into action for you.

Somewhere within you is the correct answer to every problem in your life. Somewhere within you is the power to live, and somewhere within you is the faith to believe. You are Aladdin. God has already given you the light. The genie will spring forth at your command, and you can enter into the good you desire if you believe you can.

Do you think this is too much to expect of life? Does it seem too wonderful to be true? The first steam driven boat to cross the Atlantic carried in its cabin a treatise explaining just why it was impossible for a boat to be powered by steam. Jesus said, "I am come that they might have life, and that they might have it more abundantly." No, it is not too much for you to believe that Jesus knew what he was talking about. And so, Aladdin, don't be afraid to rub your lamp. This lamp is the gift of life to you. Accept and use it!

IDEAS CONTROL
YOUR DESTINY

Ideas really control the world, because the world acts the way it thinks. But what is an idea? It is not something you eat or drink or wear. An idea isn't a physical location to which you go. An idea is a mental state.

We are familiar with the term *ideology* as it applies to individuals and groups, nationally and internationally. The struggle that is taking place in the world today is a drama of ideas that leads to human conduct in the life of the individual and in the life of a nation. Ideas are contagious. They start in the minds of individuals and groups and gradually spread until the whole world is influenced by them.

For instance, Jesus had the idea that God is right where you are, that there is a law of good available to you wherever you may be. It was this idea, that the realm of heaven is at hand here and now and may be entered into, that made him different from others. He gathered around him a few simple people who accepted his ideas, and these people gradually spread them throughout the world. They were ideas of love, of our unity with God, of the parenthood of God and the

44

community of humankind.

Mahatma Gandhi influenced hundreds of millions to believe in a spiritual force in people's lives. America's ancestors conceived the idea of a nation bound together by mutual consent through a code of laws and ethics, which we call constitutional government. The United States Constitution, with its amendments, is a grouping of ideas first conceived in the minds of people of great mental and spiritual stature.

The Declaration of Independence and the Constitution of the United States are two of the greatest human documents ever written. They really are ideas leading to a way of living together under laws that the majority agrees are for the greatest good of the largest number. Just as there flowed out of the ideas of Jesus the whole philosophy and conduct of Christianity, so there flowed from the ideas of our ancestors something that has produced the most nearly perfect system for human life that the world has yet conceived.

Henry Ford had the idea of a mass-produced automobile, crude in its beginning, but out of it comes much of our modern transportation. Someone got the idea of the steam engine. Franklin had the idea of catching power from lightning, and people like Edison and Marconi and others perfected this. Today, we wouldn't know how to live without them.

Always, someone pioneers the field of ideas. Our laboratories are places where people work out ideas. Every advance in science is the working out of ideas. Every invention starts with an idea in the mind of the inventor. Every novel represents the creative idea of its author, and your life and mine are made up of our ideas—ideas that ride into action through our conduct. Ideas really control the world. How necessary it is, then, that our ideas should be sound, that they should harm no one and do good to all.

Where do all these ideas come from? We say they come out of

the mind. They come through our thinking. But do they really come out of our mind, or is the individual mind a channel through which something greater works?

All the discoveries and inventions that make modern life comfortable have to do with natural laws that are present everywhere. Ideas are more than something inventors think up. They are something they "feel out," as though they were thinking from nature itself. This is a conviction, which many inventors have, that ideas exist in the universe and that we pick them up or draw them out of the universe, as though we were surrounded by an infinite mind that knows all things and that is always pressing against us, trying to acquaint us with these ideas. This is the explanation why truly great people are never stupidly egotistical. It is because they know and understand that they are only channels for a greater source of wisdom.

But there must be a way through which these ideas come. There must be an intimate and personal relationship between the universe and each individual. Emerson said that everyone is an inlet to the universal mind, and because they are an inlet, they can, if they wish, become an outlet to it as well. As a great scientist once said, "We think the thoughts of God after God."

Suppose we take the attitude that God is right where we are, that the mind of God contains all ideas and isn't some far away dream, but a present reality. If we are surrounded by a mind that knows everything and a power that can do anything, how are we going to make our thought a channel through which this mind may flow into creativity?

We would start by accepting that the same mind that creates everything is also creating through us, and that we may use it. This would have to become a fundamental conviction. We should have to have a positive faith in it. We would have to develop an imagination that conceives of the universe as being alive and awake and aware. We would have to accept this in the intellect and feel it in the heart.

The imagination plays an important role if we wish to live creatively. We should couple imagination with faith. We should believe that the answer to all our problems already exists in the divine mind, and we should act as though this were true. To feeling we should add faith, and to faith we should add works.

We do not wish to become idle dreamers. We want to make our dreams come true. We all wish a more abundant life, so let's see how this works out in actual practice.

Suppose someone was to come to you and say, "I don't feel that I am getting much out of life. I find myself more or less alone and friendless. I am not much of a success, and I find that much of the time I am depressed and unhappy." You would begin by explaining to them that they aren't unhappy over the laws of nature. They already accept that the law will work for them or anyone else. They already have a deep faith in invisible powers that hold everything in place.

Next, they should be made to realize that nature never lacks anything, that This Thing Called Life is already filled with limitless possibilities. They are surrounded by a creative mind that flows into everything. They already believe this about the more obvious laws of nature, such as the law of gravity. Now, they have to add another idea to their conviction, which is as simple as this: their mind is connected with the mind of God. They belong to the universe in which they live. It wishes only that which is good for them. It wills only that which is good for them, and, moreover, it knows only that which is good for them, and they must understand that this, too, is a law.

Just as they have learned how to use physical laws, so they can learn how to use mental and spiritual laws. The physical laws are already there, and the mental and spiritual laws are already there. You will have no trouble in convincing them of this, because you have used an illustration that is so very definite and easy to understand. You are using an illustration that their will, imagination, and feeling agree with.

You are going to show them that they are surrounded by a divine intelligence, which, if they permit, will flow through them. Nine times out of ten, they will accept this. But in spite of all this, they may say, "I do feel myself to be without inspiration. I do feel alone in the world. I do feel discouraged. I don't know how to live successfully."

Somehow, you have got to instill the same faith in them that they have in nature. You have got to arouse their imagination to a point where they will be willing to experiment with themselves. You are going to say, "Just imagine yourself to be what you would like to be. Try to have the same kind of faith in the guidance of divine intelligence that you have in the law of electricity." Say to them, "Look around and see how intelligence governs everything. You can see that there is an infinite mind holding everything together, otherwise nothing would be here."

You must make them feel that this mind is their mind now. They have a partnership with it. They must establish the same kind of faith in the reality of this mind that they have in the reality of other things in life. You are arousing their imagination so that they will feel this.

Now you must arouse their will to act on it. Instead of thinking of themselves as poor and weak and unhappy and forlorn, they are imagining themselves to be successful, happy, strong, radiant, alive. You must arouse their imagination to the acceptance of a power greater than they are, just as all forces in nature are greater than they are. There are mental and spiritual powers, and they are going to use them just as they would use other powers in nature.

Show them that they cannot hope to think two ways at once and meet with any great success. They will have to persevere. They must be willing to work with their thoughts, gradually bringing them under control.

You will have to convince them that belief and faith act like a law.

They are laws, and they follow rules of their own just as definitely as other laws of nature. You are going to show them how to use their imagination and feeling to play a new role in life. They are going to set up an ideal for themselves and mentally identify themselves with that ideal. When thoughts come that deny this, you are going to show them that if one kind of thought produces a certain effect, the opposite thought will produce an opposite effect.

You must teach them to have patience with themselves, as though some inner guidance within them takes them by the hand and lifts them up when they fall, as though some wise counselor within them says, "This is the right road to follow." They will have to have patience with themselves and gently, though persistently, acquire the habit of controlling their thinking.

If you do this and they follow the few simple rules you lay down, and you help them over the rough spots, it will not be long before there will be enough proof of the truth of what you are saying to build up that great hope within them that is necessary to all achievement, to build up an expectancy that has learned how to believe in the power greater than they are.

They are now in a position to receive new ideas. They are now in a position to let new things happen to them because they are keeping their mind open to the greater good and the larger possibility.

Whether you are doing this for yourself or helping someone else, you will find it the most exciting and interesting experiment of your life. In helping someone else, you will discover a new possibility and a great truth: that we are made both to live and to give.

Perseverance Pays Off

I want to tell you about a person who maintained an orphanage through perseverance and faith, a person who had a complete conviction that, no matter what was needed, when he prayed, the need would always be met.

One day, the manager of the orphanage came to this person and said that the orphanage had no food for the children's dinner. Our friend, who believed in prayer, said that he would ask God for food, and retired to his room and prayed.

About thirty minutes before mealtime, the steward again came to him, saying, "There is no food." Then, this person of faith followed the advice of Jesus. He persevered in his belief that food would be provided, and in time. He told the steward to go out and get ready for the food that would be there. In a few moments, a wagon loaded with provisions came tearing up to the door, and the children enjoyed their regular evening meal.

Millions of dollars came to this institution during the lifetime of this one man as a direct result of his persevering prayer. His life was filled with miracles of faith. Why couldn't you and I exercise the same belief in God and get the same results? Surely, This Thing Called Life will not give to one and withhold from another. Jesus said that God causes the sun and rain to come alike on the just and the unjust, and Isaiah exclaimed, "Whosoever will may come." It is not God's reluctance but our acceptance that we should watch.

Here was a person who would never permit himself to doubt. Perhaps, early in his experience, there were times when his prayers did not find fulfillment. But unlike most of us, he persevered. He was like the woman Jesus told about who came to a judge in the middle of the night to ask for help. She rapped at the door, and the judge told her to go away and come back in the morning, that he and his family were in bed and didn't wish to be disturbed. But the woman paid no attention whatsoever. She kept on rapping until finally, in exasperation, the judge opened the door and attended her needs. Jesus was the wisest person who ever lived, and he wouldn't have told us this story unless it had a meaning for all of us. The woman's persistence was an act of faith, a complete conviction that whatever is right ought to be, and can be.

Thomas Edison would try hundreds of experiments with certain ideas, and when one failed, he would merely say, "I am that much nearer the answer. If I have failed to arrive at it, it makes no difference. At least I am that much nearer the goal. Somewhere along the line I will find the answer." This was one of the great secrets of Edison's success. He exercised limitless patience. But this patience was not with the laws of nature. It was not with This Thing Called Life at all. The patience Edison exercised was with himself. He knew the law was there, and that in the split second when he obeyed it, it would answer.

I have known a number of people who did what has been called "praying through." That is, they kept right on praying until they got an answer. Perseverance and persistence are as necessary to the development of faith as they are to other experiments with the laws of nature. The late Alexis Carrel said that faith acts like a physical law in that it is a law of cause and effect.

He became a great scientist through his faith and technical skill. He not only sought divine guidance, but he found it, and you may be certain that he didn't find it immediately. Like Edison, he must have gone through a period of trial and error, of accomplishment and failure, until finally one thing stood out boldly in his mind: There is a power for good in the universe that anyone can use.

Carrel said that, above most anything else on earth, the world needs groups of people who will create great pools of faith. The late Dr. Steinmetz, an electrical genius, said that the next hundred years will develop a knowledge of the laws of mind and Spirit that will far out measure the discoveries of the last seven thousand years.

At Duke University, researchers have been scientifically testing the transcendent powers of the mind. In some of these investigations, they have tried thousands and thousands of experiments. Finally, they are bringing certain facts to light about the mind that up until now have been looked on as being absurd. This is all done in a psychological laboratory under test conditions. At last, the world is beginning to accept the results. They are bringing something new to all of us, new and wonderful.

Why, then, shouldn't you and I set up a laboratory of thought in our own minds and see what we can do with the power greater than we are? You won't need any elaborate equipment for this, because This Thing Called Life has already furnished your laboratory with all the instruments it will ever need. Life has already given you the power. It is yours to use. You already possess the pearl of great price.

Abraham Lincoln, one of the world's great souls, would have well understood the patient and persistent efforts of people like Edison,

Steinmetz, and Carrel. No dramatists have ever depicted a character more plagued by failure, nor one more blessed with the gift of persistency. Lincoln entered business and failed. He ran for the United States Senate and was defeated. He applied for an appointment to the United States Land Office and was rejected. He ran for the Vice Presidency and lost, and yet in the end became one of America's greatest presidents and one of the world's greatest statespersons.

Take then, the lesson of these people. What if you do have memories of failure and doubt? They are only experiments that didn't work out right. Why shouldn't you, too, have the same conviction that Edison, Steinmetz, and Jesus had? What if there have been wasted places in your life? There is no use crying over spilled milk, because the delivery person will be bringing another bottle in the morning.

Life comes new and fresh when the sun of hope rises to dispel the darkness of fear and uncertainty. Sooner or later, faith will count its string of pearls unto the end and find the symbol of the age—the union of humankind with God.

Why not get busy in your laboratory of thought, using the instruments This Thing Called Life has placed there: hope, faith, trust, love, perseverance, courage, and confidence? They are the gifts of God to you. Since this laboratory is in your own mind, it is always with you. The Bible refers to it as the secret place of the Most High within you, and "they that dwell in the secret place of the Most High will abide under the shadow of the Almighty."

Here is sufficient inspiration for your experiment. Life has cast the refreshing coolness of its shadow across everything on earth. There is an oasis in every desert. There is a rock in every weary land that shelters and refreshes with cooling draughts from heaven. The act of faith is so simple, so direct, so childlike in its approach, an act of belief, and if at first you don't succeed, try, try again. Life itself will never let you down.

This law of good surrenders its whole power to you when you use it rightly. It is simple enough to know whether you are doing this. All you need ask is, "Am I using this law to give more life to myself and others and in such a way as to rob no one?" This good includes your personal life as well as that of others.

This law wouldn't exist unless it was supposed to be used. People of great faith have demonstrated that the law of good exists and that it may be used. So you may begin your experiments with complete confidence. The laboratory is set up, the instruments are in your hands, and you are going to use them.

Let's imagine that you are a fine surgeon who finds it necessary to remove some obstruction from the physical body. You go about your work in confidence, knowing that when you do remove the obstruction, nature will produce a healing. Perhaps there is a little pain in the process, but you are looking to the ends, not the means. Let the patient lie quietly in bed for a few days, doing whatever is necessary under the doctor's care to comply with the laws of nature. All will be well. You are dealing with the great physician, because you are dealing with life itself.

What are some of the things that you must remove with your instrument of faith? Perhaps one of the great obstructions is the doubt of your ability to use faith, because it is not a doubt about faith itself. What you doubt is not the possibility of faith, but your ability to use it.

Like a good physician, let us diagnose the case. What is faith, anyway? Stripped naked and bare, it is a state of mind, a certain but definite way of thinking. Thoughts are things in a very literal sense. If a thought of doubt is a barrier, a thought of faith will remove that obstruction.

Faith is the instrument in your hands, the physician to yourself, which enables you to cut away the barriers of doubt and fear. Just as the woman beat on the door until the judge opened it and the man received food for the orphanage, so your thought of faith can break down the barriers that appear to obstruct your hope and confidence in life.

It doesn't make the slightest difference what your past has been or how many times you may have failed. Life itself cannot fail, and it won't fail you. If you have tried a thousand times, remember that scientists sometimes try their experiments many thousands of times. So can you.

Just as scientists know that there is an immutable law of nature on which they are depending, so you may be certain that there is an immutable law of God on which you are depending. Somewhere along the line, you will succeed. You cannot fail. Gradually, as the thoughts of doubt, fear, and uncertainty are removed and their influence fades away into the nothingness from which they came, you will find faith, like a star of hope shining brightly across your pathway.

Psychosomatic Medicine
and the Power of Prayer

In the field of psychiatry and in the medical profession, things that a few years ago would have been thought ridiculous are now being accepted by some of our best physicians and surgeons.

We all wish to be well in order that we may be happy, but a prominent physician adds that we will have to become happy if we wish to be well. There is a definite relationship between health and happiness, and since happiness is a state of mind, there is a definite relationship between our mental states and our physical well being.

This relationship is called *psychosomatics*, and we should know its basic principles if we wish to assist the physician and the nurse, whose business it is to help us to keep well physically. The word *psychosomatic* is taken from two Greek words—*psyche*, meaning mind, and *soma*, meaning body. Therefore, psychosomatic medicine means establishing a right relationship between our thinking and our bodies.

It is now accepted that many physical ailments are a direct or an indirect result of habitual thought patterns. This does not mean that a person having a stomach ulcer was expecting to have it. But it might mean that a deep-seated sense of insecurity could produce such a physical condition. Disease is not an illusion, but no doubt a larger percentage of it than most of us realize is a result of our thinking. No one can straighten out our thinking for us but ourselves. Physicians can tell us how we ought to think, but they cannot think for us. This Thing Called Life is something that we have such an immediate relationship to that no outside person can interfere with it.

What we want to discover are the few fundamental emotional states that have the wrong effect on our bodies, and we will find that they are really few in number, although their effects are multiple. They will always have a direct relationship to our reactions to life itself, to what we are doing, and to those around us.

We cannot escape living. We cannot escape This Thing Called Life, and This Thing Called Life means God, the Spirit within and around us. For instance, Carl Jung has said that faith and a belief in the reality of our own soul are the best possible mental hygiene. Another prominent psychiatrist has said that it is almost impossible to discover exactly where the emotional state leaves off and its corresponding physical condition begins. Body and mind are so interrelated that we can no longer separate them. This is the basis of psychosomatic medicine, or body-mind relationships.

Karen Horney, one of the leaders in this field, said that at the core of every neurosis, which accounts for a large percentage of wrong body-mind relationships, there are generally four fundamental propositions that must be taken into account: first, a sense of rejection; second, a sense of guilt; third, a sense of insecurity; and fourth, a sense of anxiety. The first is an emotional sense of not being wanted, needed, and loved. The next is an unconscious sense of guilt, which is followed by a sense of insecurity, uncertainty, and anxiety.

Let us start with the first negative emotion, which is a feeling of rejection, of not being wanted and loved. It leads us right back to our relationship with life and with people. We speak of certain people as being anti-social, being moody, staying too much by themselves, not having the ability to enter into the game of life and play it with joy. Such people stay alone a great deal and brood over their unhappiness. They haven't yet discovered the fundamental relationship between themselves and the world in which they live. They lack faith and confidence in people, in life, and in themselves. This has a depressing effect on the whole body and is the cause of much physical fatigue and the slowing down of the whole physical process.

Such people cannot go back over their lives and live them over again because that would be impossible. But they can rethink their experience. They can readjust their minds to the thought that people do wish them well, that they really are wanted, needed, and loved. Those who do this the best are those with the deepest spiritual conviction. By spiritual conviction I mean those who have the greatest faith in This Thing Called Life, in God.

There is nothing in the mind that hasn't been put there, and if we have felt that life rejects us, we must now reverse this process and begin to feel that we are one with it, that it desires only that which is good for us. It wants us to be well and happy. This deep-seated conviction must be rooted in faith, and there is no substitute for faith.

Psyche is the Greek word for mind, and *soma* is the Greek word for body. But there is another word, *pneuma*, which means the Spirit. It was the Greek's conviction that the individual person is Spirit, mind, and body, and that the three are interrelated. This point must be carefully considered in dealing with body-mind relationships. It is only when we put the three together that we have the whole person, because everyone is rooted in pure Spirit, whether they know it or not. If we wish to establish the best relationship between the mind and body, we must first begin by establishing the best relationship between the Spirit and the mind. The mind has to get its patterns from

58

somewhere, and all of our unconscious thought processes are fundamentally based in our relationships with the universe, with God. We cannot escape this.

If a sense of rejection is fundamental to much of our physical trouble, then we must supply it with a sense of acceptance. We must come to feel that life needs us, otherwise it wouldn't have put us here. We must come to have confidence in life. This confidence is established through prayer and meditation, through conscious communion with the Spirit. All art, all wit, and all science is useless without this relationship. The very fact that we are alive is proof enough that we are rooted in that which is life, in God, and the sooner we recognize this, the better it will be for us.

We overcome a sense of rejection by having confidence in life, by having faith in God, and by actually believing that God is within and around us, desiring our good. In such degree as we arrive at this, we will find the sense of rejection slipping away from the mind, and with it, the unconscious sense of guilt that has been harbored like an enemy within the mind. The sense of guilt can easily produce physical stagnation. It devitalizes and it depresses, and this affects the whole physical organism.

Perhaps this is why Jesus often forgave people before he performed the healing miracle of love. Love alone casts out fear. I have never yet known a person who came completely to forgive themselves and to establish a right relationship with God who did not at the same time forgive everybody else. Most of our criticism of others comes from an unconscious rejection of the self. This fact is well established. If we were to meditate daily on the thought that God loves us and that This Thing Called Life needs us, and then include everyone else in our meditation, we would soon find ourselves setting up a right relationship with all other people. Not only would our sense of guilt and rejection disappear, but our condemnation of others would also disappear.

We have covered the first two points. Now let us consider the next two, which seem fundamental to right body-mind relationships: insecurity and anxiety.

It is believed that a feeling of insecurity affects the digestion and circulation and can even produce ulcers and various other forms of internal disorders. Anxiety and strain can affect the whole circulatory system and even produce serious heart ailments. How important, then, that this should be relieved through confidence and faith in life.

How can we feel insecure if we have faith in God? The answer is simple enough: We cannot. As faith in life is restored, the sense of insecurity withers and dies. It is the unconscious feeling of insecurity which produces most of our anxieties, those vague feelings that things are not right which make the future look dark and gloomy and rob the present of its happiness. Anxiety disappears as faith enters, just as light dissipates darkness.

Someone might say, "Now you are getting back to religion again, and we wish to be philosophical, scientific, strong, and so self-reliant." Let me ask this: Is it possible for a tree to flourish when its roots are destroyed? Just so, it is impossible for us to exist in happiness and wholeness unless we recognize the greater life in which we are rooted—the life that lives in all of us and finds individual expression through you and me.

It seems as though it were impossible to have radiant physical health without right emotional balance. It seems equally impossible to have a right emotional balance without first establishing spiritual equilibrium. It is not enough to say that we came from God, because this is too vague a statement and should be followed with the thought that we now live in God. It is not enough to say there is one life and that life is God, because this thought is completed only when we add to it "God's life is my life now."

Let us keep it as simple as this, because out of the many books written on the subject of psychosomatics, we gather only a few basic facts as we seek to establish the right relationship between the mind and the body, and they are as fundamental as life itself. This is what they add up to: If we want to be well, we must first be happy; if we want to be happy, we must have confidence; if we want to be confident, we must have faith. This faith must be so deep-rooted that nothing can shake it. But how can we have such faith unless we have conviction? There must be a fundamental conviction in a power greater than we are, and we must learn to have complete reliance on it.

The funny thing is that we all have what we are looking for. It was put there by This Thing Called Life. You and I have it. Everyone has it. We just haven't been using it, because there is a center in everyone's life that is rooted in pure Spirit.

Take time each day to learn to be at home in this center. It will be the best time you ever spend. Realize that life is for you and not against you. No matter how dreary the past may have been, the future can be bright with hope and the present a thing of joy. Life comes to us new and fresh each day. We are like children who have misspelled a lot of words and our lessons are covered with errors, but let us be childlike and take our lessons to the great teacher, that they may be wiped clean of the past.

THE MIRACLE OF EVERYDAY LIVING

The phrase "everyday living" is becoming rather common. With modern miracles of transportation and communication always before our eyes, life today gives many signs of the miraculous. Medical science artificially prolonging the beat of a heart, the wonder drugs, jet planes flying faster than the speed of sound, television—all of this phenomena might well make us feel that this is the true age of the miracle, and yet the greatest miracle of everyday living is nothing new or modern. Actually, it happened around two thousand years ago and was first discovered by that spiritual genius called Jesus.

Two thousand years ago, Jesus told his followers about a power available to anyone, to which all things are possible, and he laid down explicit rules for the use of this power. The thing that made Jesus different from others was his simple acceptance that there is a power of good available to everyone.

It was his use of this power that amazed those around him. It was the simplicity of his claim that made it hard to understand, and when he said, "It is done unto you as you believe," it seemed as though he must have been talking about some distant future, and not something that is true every moment of your life.

Jesus said that the realm of God is at hand, that this realm contains everything necessary to your well being, that This Thing Called Life waits for you to recognize its presence and use its power. Jesus placed salvation where it can be reached and entered into, here and now. His whole teaching was an affirmation of the availability of divine power.

This is exactly what we all need, because you and I know that we did not create the laws of nature. We did not set the stars in their courses or cause the sun to shine or the Earth to revolve on its axis. Suppose we start with this simple proposition: We are surrounded by a creative intelligence that acts on our thoughts just as gravity acts on physical objects. This is the key to the situation, and it is a golden key because it can unlock the doorway of opportunity to us. It can bring something new and wonderful into our experience.

We must accustom our minds to the thought that mental and spiritual laws act just like other laws in nature. Of course, no one has ever seen these laws, but did you ever see the principle of mathematics? Did anyone ever see life itself? Science doesn't claim that it sees the laws of nature. It merely says that it has discovered that such laws exist, and, through experiment, we have found out how they work.

We know these laws exist because we can use them. Don't be concerned, then, if somebody asks why the law of faith exists or what it looks like. No one would ever ask this question about any other natural law. They would merely say it exists, so why not use it?

Jesus proclaimed a law of good available to everyone. He said this law responds to your faith, and in saying "It is done unto you as you believe," he presented you with the key to the situation. It is done unto you. You don't have to do it yourself. This at once relieves you of the personal responsibility of compelling the laws of nature to work.

It is not only done unto you, it is done unto you as (let us emphasize the word "as") you believe. It is done unto you in the way you believe. This is the central meaning of the whole sentence, and no doubt it is the part we have overlooked. Every law in nature delivers its power to us in accord with the way we use it. There is a power greater than you are, and you can use it. This power reacts to your belief in it.

But Jesus added another thought to this when he said, "You ask and receive not because you ask amiss." Let us see if this is a contradiction of his first statement. A little thought will show us that it is not. Jesus was merely stating a self-evident truth. The power of God is good; it cannot produce evil. It is love; it cannot create hate. It is peace; it cannot enter into confusion. Therefore, Jesus said that while there is a power greater than you are that reacts to your belief, be certain that your belief is in accord with its nature.

It isn't your thought itself that has power. Your thought possesses no power whatsoever. It uses a power greater than you are, and this power is a power of good. When you use this power for good, it delivers itself to you. Its whole creativity is at your disposal.

Jesus was never inconsistent. He was logical as well as inspired. He not only said the law of good is at hand; he used it. And he told us how to use it. The realm of God is love, peace, joy, and happiness. There is no real restriction in the use of this power greater than you are when you use it for good.

Now let us see how to use this law. Again, we are confronted by the simplicity and the directness of the wisest person who ever lived, because Jesus said that there is a certain way of thinking, a certain kind of belief that unlocks the storehouse of God to us, and he called this faith, and he called it acceptance. He referred to it as a childlike attitude toward God, a simple trust in This Thing Called Life, a complete reliance on this power greater than you are.

Jesus was talking about your mind, your way of thinking, and in his parable of the wise and the foolish virgins, he showed that everyone has oil for their own lamp. One need not borrow from another. Just as divine providence deposited oil in the ground for our use when we should need it, so the same divine providence has deposited the wealth of God's love and life at the center of your being. But Jesus said you must keep your lamp trimmed and burning. Let the wick of your faith run deep into the oil of Spirit, and your light will shine.

At last we are getting the proposition where it can be handled. We are like people who have owned land in which great wealth is deposited but who are ignorant of the fact. We have been prospecting beyond our own property, thinking we can borrow life from others, not realizing that This Thing Called Life has already buried its riches in our own plot of ground, and this plot of ground is in our own thinking, in our convictions about life, in our faith in This Thing Called Life, and in a power greater than we are.

But it isn't enough to know that the treasure is buried in our plot of ground. We have to get out and dig for it. Perhaps this is where we fall down. It costs a lot of money to sink an oil well. It takes a vast amount of technical skill and equipment and know-how, and it takes a lot of work. But if we know the oil is there, we will find some way to reach it.

Life has deposited the riches of the universe at the center of our being, but it has to be dug up, and the shaft we must sink is in our own minds. The instruments and equipment are thoughts, and the power is faith. These, too, we possess. So we had better set up our rig and start drilling.

At times, we may encounter a granite ledge or some soft earth. We can compare these to fear, doubt, and uncertainty, to the stubborn resistance of our own minds in accepting the simple truth that Jesus so carefully laid down. The sharp instrument of faith can penetrate the most solid obstruction, bore a hole through it, and reveal the treasure hidden there for endless ages.

This is why Jesus told us to pray without ceasing. He knew the oil was there, he knew how to find it, and he found it. He made the great discovery for us, and instead of proclaiming, "Look at my wealth," as though we must borrow from him, he said, "Keep your own light trimmed and burning. The well-spring of your life runs as deep, as full and free as mine." Jesus was the great explorer, the great way-shower. Having discovered God at the center of his own being, he proclaimed the good news that the realm is at hand to everyone, to every age, to all people. The greatest of all the miracles, he showed us, was this miracle—the miracle of everyday living.

So set up your rig and begin to drill. If the machinery gets squeaky at times, lubricate it with the oil of hope, and if some of its parts break down, know there is a divine mechanic within you that can repair them. Just keep on drilling, persevering in faith. Never take "no" for an answer, and never become discouraged. The oil is there. You and I didn't put it there. It was put there by a power greater than we are.

In actual practice, this means you must control your thinking. Remind yourself, daily and hourly, that since life is for you, nothing can be against you. You really can control your thinking, and no one can do this for you but yourself. Take time each day to think about the bigness of things, to feel out the divine presence in everything, and to sense the fundamental harmony that exists at the center of everything.

Don't leave this proposition up in the air and say, "When I have time, I am going to do this." There will never come any day when you have more time than you have today. That within you which denies the good you so sincerely desire is a thing of thought. When your mind says, "This is too good to be true" or "I can't understand it "or "I have to wait to accumulate a vast wisdom," remember that the thing that is talking to you is your own mind. It isn't some outside power or force operating against you. It is your own thought.

Consciously, gently, and easily, redirect these thoughts. Rearrange them, so that for every "no" there is a "yes"; for every negative there is a positive; for every denial there is an affirmation. Have a good-natured flexibility with yourself, a calm determination to think straight, no matter what happens. You are not concentrating any force or energy; you are merely coming into an agreement with something in which you already believe.

There is no thought in your mind that you cannot change if you wish to, and behind it all is your deep conviction that This Thing Called Life wills only that which is good. There is a power greater than you are that can be used for any good purpose. You cannot fail, because it cannot fail, and "unto that presence and that power alone be glory and honor, dominion and power, both now and forever."

THE BEST HEALTH BEGINS
WITH SPIRITUAL MIND HEALING

Just as everyone wishes to be happy and successful, so everyone wishes to enjoy physical health. Today we are hearing a great deal about psychosomatic medicine, which really means body-mind relationships, and a great deal about the part that our thoughts and emotions play in our physical well being. Now, let us consider the influence of faith in our everyday lives, particularly as it relates to our physical well being.

When we speak of the part that faith and prayer play in physical well being, we are not denying that people are sick or that they need medical or surgical attention. We certainly are not treating disease as though it were an illusion, but rather trying to find out how we can best help the physician or surgeon in their attempt to keep us well and physically fit.

If we are to get the most out of life and enjoy the best possible physical health, we must learn how to combine the arts and skills of science with prayer and faith. Doctors will tell you that they prefer to have patients who have faith, and we all know that the more faith patients have in their physicians, the more their physicians can do for them.

We are more than a physical body, and you and I believe that we are more than a mental mechanism. We are also a living spirit, and just as modern psychosomatic medicine is telling us that we can hardly tell where the mind begins and the body leaves off, so we wish to consider that we can hardly tell where the spirit begins and the mind leaves off. Spirit, mind, and body are closely and intimately related with each other.

You are really a spiritual being having a mind and using a body. Life has given you a body to use, a mind to think, and a spirit to act. It is the relation of this spirit to the mind and body that we wish to consider. If we find the right relationship between spirit, mind, and body, and then see to it that the body cooperates with the mind and mind cooperates with the spirit, we will discover that physical healing can and ought to be closely tied in with faith, prayer, and spiritual meditation.

Spiritual mind healing means that we keep some part of our thought open to the influx of spiritual power, that we actually believe in it and definitely train our thought to accept the simple fact that God is right where we are and that a power greater than we are can always be called on and that it will always respond.

In actual practice, this would mean that you take a definite time each day to sense and feel the divine presence around you. In order to do this, it seems better to reduce your thoughts to a few simple statements or affirmations, such as saying, "God is right where I am," "Divine life flows through me now," "I am one with the presence and the power of the Infinite."

The spirit contains the pattern of our physical body, because we are spiritual beings right now. It is certain that you and I did not create ourselves. Therefore, we must be the result of a power greater than we are, and only in drawing closer to the nature and the action and the harmony of this power greater than we are can we hope to maintain a physical well being in the stress and strain of our everyday lives.

It is now believed that a large percentage of our physical troubles can be traced to emotional disturbances deep within the mind. These emotional disturbances arise largely from our sense of insecurity, from the feeling that we do not really belong to the life in which we live, and here is where faith plays such an important role, perhaps more important than any other one mental attitude. Faith produces calmness. It establishes a sense of being one with the power greater than we are. And it does more than this. It actually opens some place in the mind that permits the circulation of spiritual energy through the physical body.

Just as we are surrounded by physical energies that seem to be the basic fact in all life, so we are also surrounded by spiritual energies. To believe in them is not a sign of weakness, but rather a sign of a deep sense that life has implanted within all of us that we are some part of the whole scheme of things.

Jesus said that the very hairs of your head are numbered, and not a sparrow falls to the ground but that your Creator knows about it. It was his ability to see through our confusion and reach back to the spiritual nature within us that gave him the power to heal those around him. If we can come to believe that Jesus was not the great exception but the great example, if we can really come to believe that we are living spirits possessing a mind and a body, then we will have a key to the situation.

In doing this, we need not deny that we are sick or need physical help, because it isn't the denial of life in any of its forms or activities that gives us the power to live. It is not the denial but rather affirmation of the presence and the power of the Spirit in us that can help us, and so you should try to keep your mind open to the thought and consciously entertain it a hundred times a day, that it is the Spirit which is circulating through you, and since this action of the Spirit cannot be obstructed by anyone except yourself, when you do keep your mind open to it, it will automatically flow through you. This is its nature.

Let us consider some very definite mental attitudes you might entertain, because we should not keep this vague and up in the air, but bring it right down to earth into our everyday experience. If you watch yourself carefully, you might be surprised how many times every day you are denying the influx of life. For instance, when you say, "My poor head" or "My weak heart" or "My bad circulation," you are not helping matters any. All of these statements should be reversed, and for every denial, there should be an affirmation.

These affirmations should be reduced to simple thoughts and then consciously used. For instance, there is one heart, one rhythm of life, one pulsation of living in everything, and you should affirm that you are part of this rhythm. God's heart is undisturbed by the turmoil of human life, and in your thinking, you should tie the action of your heart back to this great divine heart that beats in rhythm and harmony with everything.

I have often found it helps, in working with people who need physical attention, to have them ask their doctor exactly what ought to happen physically for them to be well, because the doctor knows, and then have them make affirmations that include the thought that everything that should happen is happening. In this way, there is established a complete cooperation between physician and patient. To the doctor's skill is added the patient's faith, because what a physician or a surgeon really does is to try to keep the physical instrument in tune with life so that the natural healing currents of life can flow through it.

Perhaps a bone needs to be set or a physical obstruction removed.

This is a more or less mechanical process, and the science of surgery has perfected methods for doing this. Doctors know better than you and I do that their chief function is to assist. They know that, in the final analysis, nature does the job, and that where there is proper assimilation, circulation, and elimination, there is going to be physical well being.

What is it that they do other than to prepare the physical instrument for a better influx and circulation of that living Spirit which is already within you? They cannot, through any mechanical appliance or through any medication, restore faith and confidence. They cannot inject a sense of well being. They are in the same position that you and I are, doing everything in their power to assist a power greater than we all are, the power of This Thing Called Life to establish its own rhythm in us and perform its own function through us.

So you and I have a very definite part to play, and fortunately for us the thing we need to do is to use a power that already exists at the center of our being, a power that seems to await our recognition of it, as though we must consciously permit it to enter. This is what faith, prayer, and meditation do for us, and it is certain that no one can do this as well for us as we can for ourselves.

The best patient is the one who has the greatest faith, and the person more likely to get well and keep well is the one who daily practices using faith, through making definite statements or affirmations that prepare the mind to believe in and receive into the body the power and energy of a living presence in which we all live, move, and have our being.

You might say, "This would be wonderful if I had spent years training myself, if I had read hundreds of books on the subject and studied many systems of thought." You might say, "This would be wonderful if I could discover the secret of it," as though it were hidden and mysterious and difficult to understand. So we go right back to this fundamental thought: It is the very simplicity of the thing that keeps us from using it more effectively. It is as simple as accepting life. To believe in God is the most natural thing in the world. Indeed, it is far more natural than to disbelieve in God. To accept life is easier than to reject it, and if we train ourselves a little, it is just as easy to affirm as it is to deny. If you will only keep it as simple as this, you will soon discover its effectiveness.

Let's reduce this to a few simple methods. Suppose you don't sleep well at night, but turn and toss restlessly until finally sleep and rest seem almost impossible. I mention this because there does seem to be a great deal of need right now for calmness and composure. If you are troubled with insomnia, why not take a few moments each day to get quiet within yourself. Forget all your troubles, if you have any, and say to yourself, "I have complete confidence in life. I do believe in the presence, the power, and the activity of something greater than I am, right where I am now, today, tonight, and always. I sleep in peace, wake in joy, and live in the expectation of good. It is natural when I sleep that the restoring power of life will flow through me, regulating the action of my body harmoniously. It is natural that I should rest, that I should sleep peacefully. It is intended that I should awake refreshed and renewed in mind and body."

It isn't the particular words you use that will make your affirmation effective, but the deep, simple sincerity of your belief. You cannot divorce this from faith in life, faith in yourself, and faith in God. Your statements should be made in faith, and in a faith in something greater than you are. If you do this a few times each day, you will be happily surprised at the results.

We are also told to pray for one another, because faith reaches way beyond our personal lives and reactions and can react on others as well as on ourselves. Why don't you try this sometime for someone else, and instead of saying, "I sleep in peace and wake in joy and live in the expectation of good," say, "That person sleeps in peace and wakes in joy and lives in the expectation of good," actually believing that the affirmations you use are the truth about the person of whom you are thinking.

Remember, you are not trying to influence this person or control their mind. You are not suggesting anything to them. Quite the reverse. You are merely coming to an inward feeling about them, a feeling that rises out of your own being, a sense that the person you wish to help is also a living spirit with a mind and body. In this form of affirmation, you are thinking about them. You are not talking to them at all.

I confidently look forward to the day when the physician, the psychiatrist, and the one who believes in the conscious use of spiritual power will cooperate. Each will understand the other, and they will all find they are trying to do the same thing—the physician to the body, the physician to the mind, and the physician to the soul, all cooperating with the great Physician who alone has the power to give life.

Just as the physical body and all physical objects are operated on by a law of gravitation that holds them in place, so the mind can be operated on by a spiritual energy that is just as real as gravitational force. We are not that power, but we can use it. The power is greater than we are, but it does flow through us.

Every advance in science and in human betterment has come through a recognition of powers greater than we are and a conscious cooperation with them. It shouldn't seem any more strange to think of spiritual powers than of physical ones, and no doubt they operate in the same way, the only difference being that physical powers operate directly on physical objects, and spiritual powers operate on the mind, which, in its turn, acts through the body. It is in this way that we bring spirit, soul, and body together, and this is why the Bible says that we are spirit, soul, and body. This statement does not deny the body, but includes it in a larger system. It doesn't call for a denial either of the body or the mind, but adds to body and mind the idea of spirit.

Spiritual mind healing, then, is really the healing of the mind through spiritual methods that bring the mind into harmony with the spirit, into cooperation with its nature and purpose, and into unity with its laws. The laws of the spirit are always harmonious. It is our mind that denies them, and, in a sense, it is as though the mind, in its refusal to entertain spiritual help, bars the body from receiving an influx and a newness of life, because the mind has obstructed the circulation of spiritual energy. Let the spirit circulate through the mind, and the mind will circulate through the body.

There is an ancient Chinese fable that says that we have a physical body, a mental body, and a spiritual body, and thousands of years before it was discovered that the blood circulates, this ancient Chinese doctrine said it is impossible that there should be physical health without a proper circulation through the physical body. The fable goes on to say that there cannot be proper physical circulation in the physical body unless there is proper mental circulation in the mental body, that the two are intimately tied together.

Our ancient Chinese sage said that there is also a spiritual body, just as St. Paul said there are bodies celestial and bodies terrestrial, and the sage said that just as there must be a circulation of the mental through the physical, so there must be an equal circulation of the spiritual in the mental if there is to be a whole person.

This is the meaning of spiritual mind healing, which is not a denial either of the body or a denial that someone is ill, nor is it a denial that our thinking needs to be straightened out. It is, rather, an affirmation that just as the mind and body are tied closely together, so the spirit and the mind have an intimate relationship with each other. If we can keep it as simple as this, we will better understand what

Jesus meant when he said, "It is the spirit that quickens." We will be cooperating with all the forces of nature—the physical, the mental, and the spiritual—because they all exist, and you need not deny one to affirm the other.

We do have a physical body, and we want it to be well. We do have a mind, and we wish it to be composed. We are also a living spirit. This is the way God has made us, and neither you nor I nor anyone else can change it. We do not change the laws of nature; we may merely cooperate with them. There are great fundamental laws of love and harmony in the universe, of peace, poise, and power. They flow around us and through us like all other forces.

For some reason that we do not understand, and because of our ignorance, we have accepted the physical forces but haven't yet completely tied in the spiritual ones. Now, we need to unite the whole thing into one system, keep our head in the clouds and our feet firmly planted on the earth, while the mind maintains a balance between the two. This balance is best maintained when the mind accepts the simple fact that we live, move, and have our being in a living Spirit, and that it flows through us, as the ancient Talmud said, "closer to us than our neck vein."

THE TRUE SPIRITUAL
MEANING OF THE BIBLE

Let us think for a moment of one of those dramatic incidents in the life of Jesus, when a person came to him with an incurable disease. Turning toward this person in love and compassion, Jesus said, "Be made whole."

Let us think of another time when he multiplied the loaves and fish and fed five thousand people with an abundance left over, and when he raised Lazarus from the dead, turned the water into wine, and stilled the wind and wave. What power did Jesus have that others do not possess? By what authority did he do these things? What did Jesus know that you and I must learn if we, too, would do the same works?

The answer to this and all the teachings of Jesus is contained in the Bible, which is a book of the emancipation of humankind. There are five distinct spiritual ideas that the Bible teaches about this. These five ideas contain the story of the emancipation of humankind from the creation to the fulfillment of the Christ. These five ideas gave Jesus the understanding which enabled him to raise the dead, heal the sick, turn the water into wine, and gain victory over the grave.

The first of these five great truths is told in the story of creation, which states that God is a universal, creative Spirit, or divine presence, existing everywhere, and that we are made in the spiritual image and likeness of God and therefore have within us the power to be free.

The Bible also teaches that we are individuals and are therefore let alone to discover ourselves and our partnership with the Infinite. It tells us that in the process of this self-discovery, since we are ignorant of the creative power of our thought, we bring on ourselves the limitations that we imagine, even while we feel that some power apart from God and from ourselves is inflicting injury on us. We haven't yet learned that God is the heavenly creator of all and wishes only good toward everyone. So the Bible tells us what happens when we use the creative power of our thought rightly and what happens when we use it wrongly, and gives us the key to the whole situation and places the key in our own hands and tells us how to use it.

The second great truth was made clear by Moses, the great law-giver, because Moses told us that the word of life is in our own mouths, that we should know it and do it. The whole story of the Bible is a story of the universal creative principle and presence in which we live and move and have our being, and which also lives and moves and has its being in us. The Bible is a story of our relationship to life and to God. It shows us the supremacy of love and explains the laws through which this love is expressed.

The third great truth the Bible presents is that the divine principle is within as well as around us, and that the law of good is for our use. It is one thing to learn that there is a divine presence and an infinite law; it is something else to know that this infinite presence and universal law is in the heart and mind of each of us. In a real sense, we are co-creators with God, because, as the Bible said, God's Spirit is also in us.

The fourth great truth taught in the Bible is the fulfillment of the prophecies and the promises through the coming of the Christ.

Christ is the great physician who came to heal the world, to declare the supremacy of love, and to fulfill the hopes and the aspirations of the ages, and we should not forget that it was this great physician himself who told us, "The things that I do will you do also." Jesus took the spiritual teaching of the ages and his own inward divine revelation and made them practical. He linked heaven with earth and God with the individual, and told us clearly that the one universal Spirit is in all of us, and that there is a law of good that we all can use for any and every constructive purpose.

Today we are re-reading the sayings of Jesus with new questions in mind: What can we do about it? What does it mean to us? How can we use it?

Jesus taught us how to pray effectively. He taught us how to forgive and why we must forgive if we would be made whole. He taught us how to love, and plainly told us that we could not think rightly of ourselves, or even love our immediate families rightly, unless we equally love the whole world. Jesus taught the meaning of love. He taught us the meaning of abundance and told us that whatsoever things we need, when we pray, if we believe that we have them, we will receive them. He placed no limitation on the willingness of the Spirit or the power of the law other than our own unbelief.

By example and through word, Jesus revealed to us the fifth great truth of the Bible: Life is eternal. All people are immortal, and every one of us is on the pathway of an endless evolution. In order to prove this, he showed that he knew what he was talking about. He raised Lazarus from the dead, and he himself walked into the grave to prove that he could walk through it.

He said that he came as an example, that he came to bring us a greater peace, a deeper sense of security, and freedom from fear, and he came to reveal the eternal love, the eternal givingness, the eternal forgivingness of the divine presence that is closer to us than our very breath.

THE SECRET OF SUCCESS

I am going to tell you a true story about a man who was past sixty when he became interested in knowing more about This Thing Called Life. Shortly before this time, his daughter had healed herself of a physical trouble through prayer and faith. This set him to wondering about his own situation. At one time, he had been successful, but through a change in affairs, he had lost his business and was now driving a bakery truck.

He came to me one day and told me about his daughter's healing and said, "Why can't this power that healed my daughter do something for me?" I answered, "God can do anything." He believed in the power of prayer, and his faith was now supported because his daughter had been helped. So we worked out a very simple method of procedure for him.

We decided it would be a good thing for him to take a few moments each day to meditate and pray with this one idea in mind: "God wishes me to be successful. There is an intelligence in the universe that responds to me. There is a law of good that is able to do anything.

God is right where I am; therefore, I do not have to go anywhere to find God. The law of good is right where I am; therefore, I do not have to go in search after it. I live and move and have my being in this divine Spirit and this perfect law. I believe it will respond to me; therefore, I am going to trust it."

He was now trying to accept the answer to his prayer, even though he had not yet experienced its fulfillment. As Jesus said, "When you pray, believe that you have, and you will receive." Let us say you had a garden plot and seeds to plant in it. You believe the soil could produce the desired crop. You have complete confidence in the creative ability of life, but you hadn't actually planted the seed. You are hoping for a crop without having first complied with the law of nature which says, "Plant the seed, and let the law of good do the rest."

Or say you are a person who has a hen and a dozen good eggs, and you want to raise some chickens. Somehow or other, you have to get the hen and the eggs together. The eggs are willing, the hen is willing, and you are willing, but if you keep the hen in the yard and the eggs in a basket, nothing will happen. It is necessary to put the eggs under the hen, because the hen knows what to do with them. It just sits on them for twenty-one days, rolls them over once in a while, and contemplates the happy event that is to take place.

The hen doesn't know how to make a chicken any more than you and I know how to create a cabbage, but by some divine guidance, it knows how to sit on them, as though it were guided by God's intelligence, which, of course, it really is. The hen obeys this divine urge within and sits, and sure enough, in due season, life stirs inside the shells and the little chicks come forth ready to start the business of living on their own.

You and I are not chickens or eggs, but we could learn a lot from the hen, because it simply sits on an idea until it takes form. Have you and I ever sat on an idea consistently for twenty-one days without ever leaving it? Have we rolled it over each day in our imagination, like the hen does the eggs, in happy anticipation of what is going to happen?

It was exactly this that our friend needed to learn about and to do. He already had the makings, so to speak. He merely hadn't put them together correctly. He already had the hen and the eggs with his belief in prayer and his confidence in the power. He just hadn't got the eggs under his hen.

As I said before, the eggs were willing and the hen was willing, and so was This Thing Called Life, the power greater than he was. What he had to do was to place his faith in a relationship to this power that would make it possible for the law of good to do a definite thing for him.

This man "sat on his eggs" for three months before anything happened. But he did sit on them and roll them over in his imagination every day. He had a quiet period each day when he definitely dedicated and prayed and generated faith and conviction and came to a complete acceptance. He was waiting in faith, waiting on the law of good, and resting in the knowledge that God never lets anyone down. I used to ask him from time to time, "How is it with your faith? Are you anxious? Do any doubts come into your mind?" And he would always say, "No, I am sure something is going to happen."

Sure enough, one day when he was making a delivery at a retail store, the owner said to him, "I have been thinking about you a lot lately. I need someone to help me in my business. How would you like to join me?" This our friend took as the first sign, the first leading of the Spirit to a definite conclusion, and he answered, "This happens to be the kind of business I used to be in. I understand it, and I would be happy to accept your offer."

There was another period of several months during which he worked for the owner of the store. Then one day the owner said, "I wish to retire. I want to turn this whole business over to you. You can take your time paying for it. It is a successful business; it will pay for itself."

Naturally, the man accepted this generous offer, and he himself became the owner of the business and ran it for many years, successfully. But he always had this thought in mind: "This is God's business. A power greater than I am is directing it. I am in partnership with this power."

This is a simple and true story of something that actually happened. Just one among hundreds of similar stories. Just the simple story of someone who was willing to sit on an idea for three months because he didn't know what else to do, because he believed and was persistent in his faith, because he trusted where he could not trace. This is what faith is.

There are several viewpoints we can take from this story. We can say, "Well, it would have happened anyway" or "It was just chance or good luck" or "Perhaps this story applied to this person alone, but what meaning does it have for me, because I don't want a store?" or "I have problems much greater than this person's." Yes, perhaps you have, but do you think your problems are too great for a divine intelligence to solve? Do you think the power that controls everything finds it more difficult to hatch out a planet than it does to hatch out an egg?

Jesus used one power—and only one—to heal the sick, raise the dead, and multiply the loaves and fishes. He didn't say it is big in one place and little in another. Our friend kept faith with himself and with the law of good, and he took definite time every day to meditate, to pray, to accept. He didn't even know what the law of good was going to do for him, or how or when or where. Daily, he gave thanks for what he couldn't see. Daily, he believed that a way would be opened before him.

Surely he had the faith of a little child, and how much you and I need this childlike acceptance. We all have problems. We are not different from each other, because we are all human beings. We all wish to be happy and whole, and the most interesting thing about it all is that everyone of us has faith. It is born with us. It is just as much a part of us as our hands and feet. We just haven't been using it correctly, that is all.

So let's get a hen and some eggs and see if we can't put them together. Let's take some definite ideas and stay with them in complete acceptance. Let's take all of our wants and needs to the divine source that alone can meet them, and let's believe that it *will* meet them.

I have no secret to tell you. I have no power to give you. Just forget all about me. I have just told you a simple story about a power you have access to, about a law of good waiting to be used, and about a simple approach to it that you and only you can make.

I am not giving you something, because I have nothing to offer. This thing I am talking about is life itself, which already has given to you and to me the intelligence to know, the power to do, and the faith to believe. What are you going to do with this wonderful gift of life? That is up to you. When once you recognize that fact, life will then begin to unfold for you, and the power and the glory of the realm will embrace you in your every thought and action.

Take the High Road to Happiness

Permanent happiness comes only from an inner sense of certainty that cannot be shaken. The mind must reach a place where it no longer remembers the past with anxiety or looks into the future with uncertainty. If you believe in God, if you believe in your own soul, then no matter what situation confronts you, you can be happy.

The will of God for you is the will of a boundless life flowing through you. It is the will of joy, of success, of happiness, of peace, of abundance. It is the will of the realm of heaven, not absent from this earth, but imperfectly seen. While it is true that suffering exists in the world, that poverty and unhappiness have been the common experience of humankind, it would be an unwise person who would ascribe these negations to the divine will. Those who would deny you the privilege of having the things you so earnestly desire in this world hope themselves to receive them in the next life.

When the prodigal was in a far country, destitute, nothing had happened to the divine abundance. His father's house had not been dismantled. The celestial garden still produced the fruit of the vine.

But the prodigal's face was turned, his eyes were closed, his ears were stopped, his consciousness was numbed. He had to come to himself. In coming to himself, he met, face to face, the heavenly presence that pervades all. He was enfolded in the arms of love. A banquet was spread before him. There was feasting, enjoyment, reconciliation.

Where had God been all this time? God had not been anywhere. The Divine is always present and appears wherever recognized. As you enter more completely into conscious union with life, you will realize that the universe holds as much good for you as you can take, that you can take only what you give. You cannot draw love into your consciousness through hate. You cannot draw peace from confusion. You cannot see beauty through ugliness, nor hear harmony while your ears are filled with discord.

You rob no person when you discover your own good. You limit no person when you express a greater degree of livingness. You harm no one by being happy. You steal from no one by being honestly prosperous. You hinder no person's evolution when you consciously enter into the realm of your good and possess it today.

But it is certain that you will have to love your neighbor if you wish to be happy. Your union with God implies your union with everything that lives. Do not be afraid of this. Do not shun the thought of it. Divine union means union with everything. This does not mean that you love those who are closest to you any less; you merely love all humanity more.

Think for a moment about the few whom you feel are near and dear to you. Now permit your imagination to include more. Say to yourself, "What would it be like if these few whom I love so much were multiplied, so that finally everyone I meet should arouse in me the same deep affection?" Dare to lose your small love, and you will find it increased and multiplied a million times through greater union.

Learn to be at home in the universe. No more loneliness. No more sense of isolation. See God in everyone—the same God with a different face, the same animating principle with a different form, the same divine everything—using such an expression as this: "I am consciously aware of the one presence and the one life that fills everything, lives and moves through everything, and unites everything in one common good."

The Spirit is neither sad nor depressed. If you would catch the vision of the joy that should be yours, you must dry your tears. You must lay aside your fears. You must think from that inspirational center within you which is nothing less than the Divine in you singing its song of life. The wick of your individual life runs deep into the oil of pure being. No matter what confusion appears at the surface of your life, there is always a place of calm at the center of your being. No matter how turbulent the waves may be on the ocean of your experience, there is a changeless peace beneath.

When you become confused, stop and listen to your inner calm. Turn from the confusion to that deeper something within. You will find that the confusion disappears. The light that the storm seemed to have extinguished again becomes steady. Peace comes from a sense of union with the whole. Confusion comes from a sense of separation. Confusion comes because you are looking only at the surface.

If you put a straight stick in a pool of water and then ruffle the surface of the pool, the stick will appear bent. It is not bent, however. It is merely a disturbance at the surface of the water that causes it to appear bent. If you swim underwater, beneath the disturbed surface, and open your eyes, you will see a straight stick. The bent stick was only an illusion.

So it is with confusion. It exists as a condition but not as a reality. The mirage is in your own consciousness. If confusion comes, take your intellect and dive deep into your pool of peace. Through an act of faith, open your eyes, and you will see that there is no confusion. You will discover that the confusion was in your own mind, not in the things you were looking at, because there is a pattern of perfection at the center of your being that has never been touched by disease or misfortune.

You are to know that good keeps you in perfect activity, surrounds you with love and friendship, and brings the experience of joy to everything you do. You are to impart an atmosphere of confidence and faith which uplifts and enlightens everything in your environment. It is only as you live affirmatively that you can be happy.

Knowing that there is only one Spirit in which everyone lives, moves, and has their being, you are to feel this Spirit not only in your consciousness but in your affairs. You are to hold conscious communion with this Spirit in humanity. In a handclasp, you can feel its warmth and color. In the exchange of thought, you are to feel the presence of the Divine. You are to sense it its presence clothed in individual expression.

There is a fountain of life from which, if you drink, you will never thirst again. Your search is after this fountain, that you may be immersed in it. You cannot plunge into the waters of real life unless you take everyone else in with you. The universe is one system.

Say to yourself daily, "I am one with all the life there is. I am one with all peace. I am one with all good, and I desire that this good will flow through me to everyone I meet, to bless every situation I find myself in, and to bring peace and happiness to everyone I contact."

Your intellect senses this through intuition. Your imagination feels it by divine right. Your inward consciousness knows it through faith. What you are trying to do is to awaken your whole being to spiritual awareness.

That which thought has planted, thought can uproot. The conditions laid down by mental attitudes, whether or not you are conscious of them, can be changed. If you are experiencing some condition that is unhappy, you must know that there is nothing in you which attracts this condition, nothing in you that holds it in place, nothing in you that believes it must be this way. Turn your mind entirely from the condition and think in an exactly opposite manner.

Suppose you place your physical environment, including your body and your conscious mind, at one end of a line. At the other end, place your spiritual being—God and infinite possibility. At this end of the line, everything is already perfect. Jesus called this the realm of heaven that ought to come on earth. It should make its advent in your experience. It wants to. "The Spirit seeks such."

This end of the line is the realm that has been promised. This Spirit is happy, whole, free, filled with joy, eternal in its existence, and can provide you with everlasting expansion. All your highest hopes and dreams have come from it. The echo of its being is in your intellect, the voice of its unspoken word is in your mind, the feeling of its light and life is in your heart, the emotion of its imagination is in your soul.

At the other end of the line is your physical environment, including your body, most of your conscious thoughts, your daily hopes and aspirations, fears and failures, all apparently isolated, wandering in a desert of despair, climbing endless mountains, at times lost in interminable forests through which light does not break, fording rushing streams in the turmoil of life, searching, wondering, hoping, longing, yearning toward that other half of its being that alone can make it whole.

Don't you think this is a good description of your attitudes and experiences? One half of you in heaven, the other half on a dense earth. The heavenly, willing to come forward and answer your every need; the earthly, half striving toward the heavenly and the apparent barrier. If you knew, as you know that you live, that this barrier were only a thing of thought or belief, the first half or your journey would be accomplished. You would know that you have the tools to cut down the forests, level the mountains, bridge the streams, and cause the desert to bloom.

If you listen to yourself long enough, you will know this. With hope and enthusiasm, you will start on your journey. You will never become discouraged or disheartened. Your vision will be on this city of good, and your feet, your mind, your intellect, your will, will travel toward this city, and you will surely enter its gates. As you enter into life, feeling the divine presence in everything, more and more you will hear a song of joy singing at the center of your being. You have only to be still and listen to this song of life, because it is always there.

You cannot be happy unless you believe in immortality. You not only have the joy of living today, but an equal joy of knowing that you will live forever. Always, your horizons will be expanding, filling your life with new hope, new vigor, and new assurance. Life is not static. It is forever dynamic, always creating, not something done and finished, but something alive, awake, and aware. We sleep only to wake up again.

As you consciously poise yourself in the realization that you live in pure Spirit, new power will be born within you. You will find yourself renewed by the divine life, led by divine intelligence, and guided by divine love. Focus your inward vision on this indwelling harmony, knowing that as you contemplate its perfection, you will see it manifest in everything you do.

The world starves in the midst of plenty, weeps in the midst of joy. Yet, the eternal manna has never ceased to fall. The fields of God are ripe unto the harvest. The garden of your mind was planted by a wisdom superior to yours. Enter in, and possess this promised land. When you accept in simple faith, you will receive. When you knock in childlike belief, the door will be opened. What you seek with enthusiastic acceptance, you will find. Did not the great and beautiful Jesus proclaim, "Come unto me, all you that labor and are heavy laden, and I will give you rest"? Reality has not changed since Jesus walked the shores of Galilee. The power he used is still here.

YOU ARE IMPORTANT TO GOD

There is a creative urge behind everything you do—an urge to express life, joy, and happiness, an urge to reach out to everything that lives, as though you belong in the universe in which you live, to be one with it and have an enthusiastic zest for living. Humankind's nature is such that it is necessary for us to express life, to come into the fulfillment of joy and happiness, and we are disconsolate until this happens.

Not only human beings, but everything in nature is endowed with this creative urge. When moisture is precipitated, the desert receives it with gladness and breaks forth into a song of creation. Making the most of its brief season, it blossoms in joy, storing within its bosom the seed of a future flowering. It is impossible to escape this creative urge. Everything must find fulfillment or perish.

No one willed this so. Evolution is proof of an irresistible urge that pushes everything onward and upward. We did not create life; we are something that lives in, from, and by it. We cannot escape life or the necessity of giving expression to it through living. In some way that you know not of, through some process that never reveals its face, life has entered into you, and with it the irresistible impulse to create. Therefore, I am going to trust it.

Divine Intelligence has willed it so, and neither you nor any other person, nor all the wit, science, or philosophy of humankind, nor the inspiration of saints or sages, can change one bit of it any more than we can arrest the eternal circuits of time, the revolutions of the planets, or the desire of the fledgling to leave its nest, to soar and sing. "Create or perish" is the eternal mandate of nature. Being constructive or becoming frustrated is an equal demand.

Neither you nor I can escape the demand that life makes on us. We are important to God, and we do wish to live creatively. Life has made each one of us individuals. We do not all have to act or think alike, but we all should give full rein to the urge within us to express life, and since we are individuals, there must be some place within each one of us that can open up a complete current and circuit for divine love, energy, and action to flow through us into the most commonplace things of life.

We should not think of this as being hard or easy, or big or little, because the same power that holds the mountain in its place is the power that is holding you and me in the individual position we take in life. What we should learn to do is to cooperate with this power. Its whole nature is love and harmony; therefore, we will get the best results when we live together in harmony and with love for each other. Out of this love and harmony should flow a great creativity, a happy livingness, and an expectant enthusiasm.

You must expect to find this power at the center of your own being, because God works for you by working through you, and This Thing Called Life is intimate to everyone, even as the law of good is available to all. Take your place, then, in the universe in which you live. Having neither fear nor arrogance, but in the simplicity of faith, come to believe that you belong to the universe in which you live. You are one with the creative genius behind this vast array of ceaseless motion, this original flow of life. You are as much a part of it as the sun, the earth, and the air.

There is something in you telling you this, like a voice echoing from some mountain top of inward vision, like a light whose origin no one has seen, like an impulse welling up from an invisible source. Your soul belongs to the universe. Your mind is an outlet through which the creative intelligence of the universe seeks fulfillment.

This is your starting point for investigating the meaning of those impulses, longings, and desires that accompany you through life. You may accept that the source through which they come is real. You may accept that the universe is filled with a divine and infinite presence, including the infinite of yourself. Not the infinite of your limited self, but the infinite of the divine self you must be. There is a pattern of yourself in this invisible.

Suppose, with utmost simplicity, you accept the Spirit that is in you—not in the mountain, not at Jerusalem, not even in the temple, although it is there also, but in you, the spirit of yourself, the Spirit of God in you. If God created you after God's own nature (and there is nothing else God could have made you out of), then the thing you are after is already here within you.

The only things that stand between you and it are the accumulated thoughts, beliefs, and emotions of the centuries. But there is nothing there that has not been put there either by yourself or the human race. What has been put there can be removed. These unbeliefs are thought patterns laid down throughout the ages and accentuated by your own experience, by your inherited tendencies and environment. There is no use wasting time speculating as to what avenue they came through. Your job is to reject them. This great thing within you, which is called *will* or *choice*, can decide your destiny. It can remove every obstruction and gradually implant new patterns in your mind.

As an illustration, think of a tunnel, one end of which is out in the open where there are fertile valleys, glorious sunshine, verdant vegetation. There is song, laughter, happiness, peace, and joy. Let us call this the valley of contentment. Let us also call it the realm of God.

You are at the other end of this tunnel, with a surrounding view overlooking a barren desert through which no refreshing streams flow. Somehow, your attention has been drawn to the far end of the tunnel. With a curiosity that you did not put in your mind, you wish to investigate where this tunnel leads, what is at the other end of it. You peer into the tunnel. At first it seems dark, but occasionally a shaft of light shines through it and you catch a vision of the other side.

You have a great longing to walk through this tunnel, to leave behind the dismal scene of discontent and unhappiness and to enter into the joy that your brief glimpse has promised, because in this glimpse, you have seemed to see yourself standing at the other end of the tunnel. Perhaps, in this momentary vision, you seem to have seen your own spirit. It seems as though something says, "Yes, this is myself." And you say, "How am I going to unite myself with my self?" Then darkness closes in. Your vision has vanished. It must have been an illusion.

There are two voices that seem to be talking to you. One voice says, "You are following a mirage, an illusion. There is nothing real but this end of the tunnel. Accept things as they are. Make the best of them. Be as happy as you can, but do not hope." This is the voice of despair.

The other voice is saying, "Do not be afraid. Your vision is true. Enter the tunnel and walk through. There is nothing solid in it. That which obstructs your passage is vapor, the vapor of unbelief. It is dense only with the denseness of doubt. It is filled with the fears of the ages. There is a lamp within you already lighted. As you walk through the tunnel, the darkness will disappear because of this light. You will find that other half of your self, and you will discover that this tunnel is your own mind."

This is a picture of your self—your efforts, your hopes and longings, your inspirations and doubts, your fears and faiths. The barriers between you and your greater good are not barriers in themselves. They are things of thought. It is because of this that all things are possible to faith.

The freedom that the all-creative wisdom has designed for us is marvelous beyond human perception. Life has given us an intuitive sense of things. It has permitted us to evolve through countless ages of trial and error to the day of our redemption, always knowing that this redemption is certain. But the timing, even of eternity as far as we are concerned, rests in our present or delayed acceptance. It could be today or tomorrow. It could have been yesterday. We are living in a universal now, and this now waits on our acceptance.

Don't you think that even God could not have done it any other way? Can't you see that even the divine will, in ordaining your destiny, was compelled to let you work out your own future? The more you think about this proposition, the clearer it will become. Do you think it would have been possible for it to have been any other way? You would not wish to be a robot any more than you would wish to be a cabbage or a wave of the ocean or a knot on a tree.

The greatest gift life could have made to you is yourself. You are a spontaneous, self-choosing center in life, in the great drama of being, the great joy of becoming, the certainty of eternal expansion. You could not ask for more, and more could not have been given. You need not mold your life after another. Trust yourself. Believe in your direct relationship with life, and you will not be disappointed. Do not wait. Today is the time to start. Right where you are is the place to begin.

Jesus said that if you seek the realm first, everything else will be added, and in this "everything else" is included all things in this life that make for full livingness and joy, peace and happiness, health and harmony, and the success that rightfully belongs to you as a divine being. It is this divinity that you are to accept and learn to accept in all of its fullness. If you were not important to God, God would not have put you here.

This really resolves itself into a very simple proposition: God is all the power there is and Spirit is the one supreme presence in which you live. This Spirit had intelligence enough to create everything, and it hasn't gone out of business. Your business is God's business, and God's business is your business.

Think of yourself as being in partnership with this divine presence and this perfect law of good. Learn to trust it, just as you trust the simple fact that you are living. Do not be afraid to throw yourself in complete abandonment and with perfect acceptance into its soft embrace, because it is closer to you than your very breath and nearer to you than your hands and feet. It is right where you are.

GOD WANTS YOU
TO BE YOURSELF

Did you know that you are a wonderful person in your own right? Do you know that This Thing Called Life has set a unique stamp of individuality on you, and that no one else can ever take your place in the scheme of things? No two people have identical thumbprints, no two blades of grass are alike, no two leaves of a tree, no two snow-flakes are ever identical.

So often we single out some character in history or some person we know and think, "How I wish that I might be like them!" Yet, this would be suicide to the real self. If This Thing Called Life has seen fit to make us all just a little different, then we do not have to be exactly like others. If two people were exactly alike, one of them would be unnecessary in the scheme of things.

You and I are individuals, but we are individuals rooted in one life, each drawing directly from it the power, the imagination, and the will to live as an individual, as a personality of God, and to do this in a unique and different manner.

We all must learn to trust ourselves and, as far as possible, give full rein to all the creative power we have. At the same time, we must all live together as members of one human family. But unity does not mean uniformity. We can live together in harmony and with cooperation without infringing on the rights of others. This is the real meaning of democracy and personal freedom.

If a thousand artists were painting the same landscape, no two drawings would be identical, because each artist would put something on their canvas that would be individual, something the landscape told them that it didn't tell anyone else. So it is with everything we do. One of the great lessons of life is to learn to be yourself, to have confidence in the high impulses that come to you as an individual, and to know that a power greater than you are has willed you to be a little different from all the rest.

If each of us is a unique personality in This Thing Called Life, then it follows that all the power there is and all the presence there is is behind each individual. There is nothing monotonous in this great scheme of things that we call life. The power to live and the intelligence to know what to do exist at the very center of your being. You didn't put it there, and you couldn't destroy it if you tried. The sensible thing to do is to accept this and work in cooperation with your inner life. It is my personal conviction that there is a spirit of the real self that accompanies us through life, but that we are only dimly aware of it.

There is an ancient fable that says when the gods decided to create a human form and make it divine, they wished to hide the human's divinity in a place that would be difficult to discover. So they held a consultation during which one of the gods said, "Let us hide the human divinity in the air." But another one said, "No. Someday the human will build a machine and fly through the air and discover it."

Another god suggested that the human divinity be hid at the bottom of the sea, and another said, "No. We have given the human such creativity and such an imagination that someday they will invent a machine that will penetrate the depths of the ocean." And yet another one of the gods suggested that the human divinity be hid in the ground, because surely it would not be discovered there. But one of the wise gods said, "No. Humans will bore even through the earth and discover their divinity."

So after much discussion, they all agreed that the best place to hide humans' divinity, the place where the human would be least likely to look for it, would be deep within the individuals themselves. They said that humans will always be looking outside of themselves, and they will never think that the thing they are looking for will be the thing they already have. And so they hid our divinity at the very center of our own being and left us alone to discover it. But always there was the urge within us, a feeling that there is something still undiscovered, something that could make everything right if we knew how to find it and use it.

It was this divine thing within us that Jesus discovered—his intimate and individual relationship to the living Spirit. It was this that gave Jesus the power he had. All the miracles he performed and all the wonderful signs that followed his life were evidence enough that he had laid hold of a power that other people knew nothing about, and yet they already possessed this thing that they were looking for in another. Don't you think this is what Jesus meant when he told his followers that it is neither in the mountain nor at Jerusalem, but within yourselves that you will discover the real realm, the actual spark of life, the pattern of your own divinity?

How true it is that we have searched everywhere. Yes, you and I have traveled far and near and searched high and low to find that something that can make us whole and give us joy in living. Seldom has anyone realized that the wonderful person they are looking for is really the divinity hidden within them—God's good person. Isn't it true that even many of our success stories are weak examples of how we should imitate others? Do they really teach us that there is a deep self that does not have to imitate anyone?

You can read Shakespeare all your life and never become Shakespeare. You can be familiar with all the poems ever written without being able to produce three verses that are original. You can imitate all the great actors and still give a poor performance. This alone should teach us that imitation is suicide. There is only one way a person can learn to write, and that is by writing. There is only one way a person can learn to sing, and that is by singing.

You and I will have to learn how to live by living. We have lived too much by imitation. Now let's try a new experiment. Let's make up our minds that God, the supreme intelligence, has hidden within each of us the very essence of God's own being and has let us alone to discover ourselves.

First of all, we must have a conviction that there is such a real self hid behind this mask we wear. We did not implant this divinity within us. This is the gift of life. How can you possibly account for those inner strivings you have, the inward feelings that stir within you, unless they are echoes of some deep self wishing to reveal itself? It is my complete conviction that This Thing Called Life has made us individuals, and that what we call our personality is merely the use we are making of a presence within us that waits our recognition of it.

I know, just as well as you do, that the world is full of skepticism and doubt, and I realize that a lot of what we call—or *miscall*—hard-headed, practical people are apt to treat lightly the thought that everyone is divine in origin. But I am not quite sold on the idea that you can weigh everything on a scale or measure everything with a yardstick. You can kill a nightingale, but you will not have captured its song. The thing that produced Beethoven's symphonies was Beethoven himself. It wasn't some external or internal piece of mechanism. It was his own soul that projected these symphonies, and when he left this world, he took their cause along with him, even though he left behind a beautiful echo for all to hear.

You can dissect the human body, and still its life will elude you. You can analyze the brain and not find one single thought hidden there. No, you and I are not yet sold on the idea that we are an aggregate of mechanical reactions. I have never yet seen a typewriter that can, of its own accord, produce a beautiful poem, nor have I seen a printing press that can produce a Sermon on the Mount.

At the expense of being thought a little impractical by those who are so filled with common sense (or what they call common sense) that it oozes out of them like perspiration on a hot day, I think you and I will do well to remain true to a dream, a dream no analyst has ever analyzed, because it isn't a dream at all. It is the one solid and final reality about us. You are a spirit—right now. And the spirit that you are is rooted in the eternal Spirit, which is God, the living Spirit Almighty.

Intelligent physicians know they never heal anyone. They merely draw the healing power of nature through their patients. Intelligent psychologists never think that a human being, or all human beings together, creates humankind's mind. They only straighten out human thinking so that something greater than the human mind can dominate mental and emotional reactions. Physicists never create energy; they merely use it. And theologians do not create God.

So the story is told, the lesson is learned, and we would do well to heed it. Deep within us, deep within you and within me and within all people, something was planted by This Thing Called Life, planted deep within us, and is trying to come forth into the fruitage of human endeavor. You and I and all people have our roots in a deep and abiding reality. How will the rose blossom red unless it draws its being from that creativity in which it is rooted? How will one rose be different from another unless life is imparting to each some unique and individual expression of its own feeling, its own beauty, its own fragrance?

You and I would like to have that great, big, wonderful personality. We would like to be the person we have dreamed about. We have merely been looking in the wrong place. It is time for us to stop and look and listen, because we are on the crossroads of terrific human events, and everyone awaits news from the realm of God.

Who will bring it? You are the only one who can bring it to yourself. I am the only one who can bring it to myself. We are the only ones who can reveal it to each other. When I say "you" and "I" and "we," I mean that the universe and God come silent and alone to each one of us in the stillness of our own souls.

GOD AND EINSTEIN

After many years of patient work, Dr. Albert Einstein felt that he had found one law governing all physical phenomena. If so, it is one of the greatest and most important discoveries of all time. But what has this to do with This Thing Called Life, or with the possibility of using a power of good greater than you are? Well, let's see what we can figure out.

Is it any different to say that there is one law governing all physical phenomena, or to say with Emerson, "There is one mind common to all individual people"? The universe is a spiritual system. It is a manifestation of divine intelligence. Another prominent scientist has said that we can think of the universe in the terms of intelligence acting as law, which means mind in action. And another scientist has said that we can think of the universe in the terms of an infinite thinker thinking mathematically, which means that faith acts as a law, and this is why prayer can be answered.

Here is another remarkable thing: Dr. Einstein also said that time, space, and light curve back on themselves. This means that everything moves in circles. It explains what Jesus meant when he said,

"Give, and it shall be given unto you; good measure, pressed down and shaken together, and running over." It also explains another saying of Jesus when he said that they who take up the sword will perish by it. It really means that what goes out will again return, that the inner action of our mind decides what is going to happen to us, because "as we think in our heart, so it is."

I would like for us to consider one more of Dr. Einstein's propositions, in which he states that energy, which is invisible, and mass, which means physical form, are equal, identical, and interchangeable. Is this any different from one of the initial statements of the Bible where it says, "In the beginning was the word"? What we see comes out of what we do not see. The invisible becomes visible through a law of mind. This is what is behind psychosomatic medicine. Thoughts are things in that mental states produce definite results. This is why we meditate, pray, and affirm the presence of good in our lives.

The cause of everything is hidden. What we experience outwardly is a result of silent but intelligent forces that operate on the invisible side of life. As far as you and I are concerned, our minds represent this invisible side of life. Another great scientist, Dr. Gustof Stromberg, said in his book, *The Soul of the Universe*, that there is an invisible pattern for everything in the visible world. This is no different from the Bible statement that the invisible things of God are made manifest by the visible. Everything, including our own being, is rooted in and draws its life from an invisible source. Is this any different from St. Paul's statement that there are bodies celestial and bodies terrestrial, that there is a spiritual body as well as a physical body?

It is wonderful that so many scientists are giving us a faith in the spiritual universe, a faith that we have already had through intuition but that now is coming clearer and clearer in the mind's eye. Wouldn't it be strange if we should discover that the Bible is not only a book of spiritual inspiration, but that it also lays a spiritual foundation for many of the recent discoveries of science?

If there is one law governing all physical phenomena, then there must be one law of mind governing all mental action. And if time, space, and light bend back upon themselves, then our thought will return to us. This is why Emerson said, "If you want a friend, be a friend." And this is why Jesus said that if you want something good to happen, accept that it is happening, which implies that there is a law that brings back to you a direct result of your thinking. He said, "When you pray, believe that you have."

Science also teaches us this very important fact: Nature wills ill against no one. The laws of God are for us and not against us. It is our use of them that produces pain instead of pleasure. When we learn to live in harmony with them, they will become our servant instead of our master. This means that many of the laws we have been using destructively can as easily be used constructively. Often, our bondage is a misuse of freedom, just as much of the world today has used its freedom to destroy its liberty.

To realize this is a step toward freedom and will have a direct bearing on our health, our happiness, and our success. We will no longer feel that we are fighting a power opposed to good, but rather that we are using a good power in a wrong way. We will know that we have an ally with us, an unconquerable power of good and an irresistible law of love.

But the skeptic may say this is too good to be true. I ask you, is modern invention too good to be true? Are cars and televisions too good to be true? Are the things being worked out in modern laboratories real or unreal? There is only one answer to this: They are real enough, and we are merely discovering the possibilities of life. There are great spiritual and mental laws that govern everything, and you and I really are living in the mind of God right now. There is a power for good available to all of us.

The laboratory of our mind is a place where we test out what our thoughts can do for good or for ill. "Mind is the power that molds and makes, and humankind is mind, and evermore we take the tool of thought and, shaping what we will, bring forth a thousand joys, a thousand ills. We think in secret, and it comes to pass. Environment is only our looking glass." Life is a mirror, reflecting back to each one of us what we really are.

Life has willed it this way, and you and I cannot change it. There are only two things we can do. We can learn to live in harmony with the law of our being, or, by opposing it, live in unhappiness until, through suffering, we learn how better to use that silent force of good that flows through us, the power greater than we are but a power that is right where we are.

If we can know with complete certainty that a law of good conspires to help us when we use it, and that this law is a real law of God and cannot be changed, then we become victors, as the Bible says, through Christ who strengthens us. And *Christ* means the child of God within us, the divine pattern in which we as human beings are rooted, the perfect person that Jesus spoke of when he said, "Be you therefore perfect, even as your Creator in heaven is perfect."

Faith is the most wonderful thing in life, and we need a faith so rooted, so firm, so unshakable, that it will not waver. This kind of faith is arrived at through a conviction in the intellect and through a feeling in the heart. We need both conviction and inspiration to live happily. Without conviction, we are never sure, and without inspiration, we lack that most vital of all things—a zest and an enthusiasm for living.

Have you and I really tried God? I wonder, and I still wonder. Have you and I really tried God? Can we sit down in the midst of confusion and think peace? If all the forces of nature curve backward upon themselves, if we can think peace even in the midst of confusion, we will establish peace in our lives.

"Be still, and know that I am God." This is no idle statement. It is as profound as life itself. Have you and I really consistently, over a period of time, kept careful enough guard over our thinking to actually know what might happen when we exercise a dynamic faith? I am afraid we haven't. There is no use crying over the past. If we have been defeated, the only thing to do is to rise and strive again, but this time with a new hope, a fresh vision, and a greater certainty.

I cannot help but believe that the world is on the verge of great spiritual discoveries, that the late Dr. Steinmetz was right when he said the next hundred years of research in the realm of mind and Spirit will produce more important discoveries than the last seven thousand years of research. Let us definitely accept that we have an intimate and personal relationship with This Thing Called Life, that there actually is a power for good greater than we are that we can use, and that no one but ourselves can bar our way to a fuller life.

The one sure thing that you possess and that no one can rob you of is yourself, the hidden *you*, that something within you greater than all fate. Learn to trust yourself because you first have faith in God. Take time each day to reaffirm your intimate relationship to the Spirit. Act as though you were the child of God, and you will surely discover that you are. Inspiration, hope, and joy will come with this revelation.

This is the secret of life, the pearl of great price that you are to treasure in your innermost being even as you share it with others, because the love you have for them will come back to you multiplied, and the good you set in motion will return to you thousand fold. This is the way of life. This is the law of your being. This is what the saints, the sages, the poets, the wise, and the good of the ages have known. This is what Jesus taught. This is what you and I believe. This is what is true.

The Whole Human Family

Everyone wishes to have a friend and to be a friend, and everyone wants to be happy. Surely it is intended that we all live together in peace and prosperity, and there is a way through which this can be brought about. Let us think about some of the things we must do to bring about peace on earth and goodwill among all people.

First of all, we must do away with race prejudice, because there is really only one race, which is the human race, and while we are all different, we all belong to this one human family. We must learn to respect each other, to know of the needs of the other person, and to realize that at the base of everyone's life there is a sincere desire to love and to be loved.

There is a lot more good in the world than we realize, and it is this good in each other that we wish to bring out. Sometimes we feel that if we could change the world in a minute through some miracle of love, all would be well, and this is true. But the world is made up of the people who live in it, and that means you and me. So all of us will have to begin right where we are. You will have to begin where you are and I will have to begin where I am, right now, today.

Haven't you often met someone, just in passing, and said to yourself, "If I knew this person better, I am sure that I would admire them"? Perhaps we are just a little too timid. Perhaps there isn't quite enough give and take in life. We are all so much alike inside. We all do want people to like us, and we want to feel that we enter into others' lives in some vital way. We all have the same needs, the same hopes and longings.

It doesn't matter that we have different opinions, because we are all individuals. Each one is a person in their own right, and unity does not mean uniformity. But unity does mean that we get along as a human family. There are several hundred different churches in the United States, but they all believe in one God. We have two great political parties, but each believes in the United States. We have forty-eight States in one Union. It is not the different opinions that we need be concerned with, but how to get along with each other in one world.

The problem begins right at home, in your mind and in mine. Have we kindness for others? Are we flexible enough to know that we all don't have to think alike in order to get along? Are we able to put ourselves in the other person's place? Can we overlook the irritations of life and reach across all difference of opinion to the common ground on which we all stand and the united purpose toward which we all strive?

We all live, move, and have our being in one God. This Thing Called Life and the power greater than we are gives itself alike to everyone who receives it. Samuel Walter Foss said, "Let the howlers howl and the growlers growl and the scowlers scowl, and let the rough gang go it. But behind the night, there is plenty of light, and the world's all right, and I know it."

It is this kind of understanding that the world needs today, perhaps more than at any other time in its history. From it alone can come a mutual sense of security and well being between people and nations. This vision is a broad and deep one, and on its successful outcome depends the destiny of the world. Surely the place to begin is with the self, and we should say to ourselves each day, "Have I a little more tolerance than I had yesterday? Have I a little more understanding of other people's needs? Have I developed a little deeper sympathy? Am I better able to forgive and forget than I was yesterday?" If so, we are on the right track.

It seems as though one part of the world is trying to destroy everything while the other part is trying to sew it together again. The people who are trying to sew the world together again are those of a larger vision and a deeper faith. Today, they are the hope of humanity.

You may be certain that those who are trying to tear the world apart have only little faith in God, and those who are trying to put it together again have a deep conviction that there is a spiritual power that could operate in human affairs if we would let it. I cannot help but believe that these are the ones who will finally win. "For truth crushed to earth will rise again; the immortal years of God are its. But error, wounded, writhes in pain and dies among its worshippers."

You cannot separate what is best in the world from some kind of faith in This Thing Called Life, and somewhere along the line, what is best is bound to win. But it can win only as more and more people come to believe in it, as more and more people come to live as though it were true, and since we act the way we think, the most needed thing in the world today is that more people will come to believe in God. God is the great common denominator of the whole human family. We do live and move and have our being in a divine presence that, if we would let it, could guide us all correctly.

There is a wonderful book called *What Would Jesus Do?* which says that when we face a problem, we should first ask, "What is the right thing to do? What would Jesus have done if he had to make this decision?" And a Catholic, Brother Lawrence, who wrote *Practicing the Presence of God*, said that we should seek to find God in each other and in the most menial task of everyday living. It remained for Jesus to say, "This is my commandment, that you love one another as I have loved you."

Again, you and I will have to begin right where we are. Are we practicing the presence of God in our human relations, as though there were a good road that we all might follow that leads to mutual tolerance, cooperation, and unity? God should always be first in our relations with life. The world will have to come to this position if it is going to survive, and I wouldn't be talking to you—and I don't think you would be listening—if we didn't all feel that we have missed something that could make everything well with us and with each other. And we are right. Not right because others are wrong, but right because God is a living reality.

Our great nation is made up of millions of human beings living in one country. The world is made up of even more millions of human beings living in one world, and yet no two people need think or act alike. Each is an individual. The rosebush is not a grapevine, nor is a European an American. But the rosebush and the grapevine are rooted in one common soil. They draw their whole being from it, and the European and American are rooted in one Divine Mind that has seen fit to make each a little different, while keeping them all in its own Spirit. There is plenty of room for variety in groups and in nations—different thoughts and ideas, different ways of living, different political, economic, and cultural systems. We need this variety. But behind it all, we need a sympathy and an understanding with each other, just because we are all human beings.

It isn't necessary in the immediate family life that each member think and act alike. There may be four children, and each may go into a different profession, and this is exactly as it should be because this is the way God made us. But there is a spirit of helpfulness and cooperation in a happy family that promotes the well being of each member, permitting each to be a little different, while at the same time finding common purposes behind their united action.

So it is in the larger family of the human race. We in America have no trouble with Canada or Mexico, and yet here are three commonwealths made up of many people who live side by side. We don't say to the people of Canada or of Mexico, "You must think as we in California think or as my ancestors in New England thought." We sometimes laugh at the way our ancestors thought and feel we are doing a little better job than they did, but we still remain Canadians and Mexicans and Americans. We are individuals wherever we go.

The thing that makes for unity is that each group will respect the individual difference of other groups while at the same time cooperating with them. This is not only possible but necessary if the world is to survive. We each have an individual part in this great scheme of things, and the most valuable thing anyone of us can do today is for each to be a little more certain that we are meeting life with a deeper understanding and sympathy for others, with a greater love for all.

I don't believe that this is merely an idle sentiment or wishful thinking. It is practical. More and more of our great leaders in education, in religion, and in science are coming to accept this position, and they are right.

You and I want to take our part in the building of a better world—a world where there is peace, prosperity, and goodwill without coercion, a world where there is individual and collective security and freedom without fear, a world where there is unity without uniformity, a world where each may run as fast and as far as they wish, without interfering with somebody else.

I believe it is the destiny of our great country to preserve freedom, prosperity, and cooperation within its own borders and, in so doing, become an object lesson to the whole world. I believe it is the destiny of America to remain a democracy and, in following the leading of the Divine Spirit, to preserve human freedom—the sanctity of the individual life—while at the same time creating an opportunity for everyone.

It is the greatness of America to rise above the prejudice of race and creed, because there is only one race, which is the human race, and only one final creed, which is our common belief in God.

I believe it is the faith of America to keep this high vision always before it. This is the American spirit. I like to call it the Spirit of God in America.

THE SECRET OF THE AGES

No one can doubt that Jesus was the wisest person who ever lived. Anyone who could heal the sick, turn water into wine, multiply loaves and fish, or transform other people's lives as he did must have possessed the secret of the ages. He must have known something that others had not found out.

Jesus possessed a secret so profound, so powerful, so awe-inspiring that he became the greatest figure in human history. Jesus had knowledge of a power so great that it commanded the wind and the wave, and you and I wish to discover this secret and to make use of this power.

We must turn to the words of Jesus if we wish to discover the nature of this profound secret that he possessed. Our greatest difficulty will lie in the simplicity of what he said. Jesus had a secret so simple that all of us can understand it, a secret the knowledge of which, rightly used, can transform our lives from fear into faith, from weakness into strength, from doubt into certainty.

It seems to me that there are two basic facts or ideas about the secret that Jesus possessed, and I believe these two ideas are fundamental to everything he said and did. The first part of his secret was that God is the creator of us all. Unlike others, Jesus did not think of heaven as some remote place or far-off event. He plainly told his followers—and that means all of us—that heaven is within.

God was as real to Jesus as you and I are to each other, so close that we need not go in search after God, because the secret place of the Most High is already at the center of our own being. Jesus talked to this divine presence within and around him as intimately as you and I speak to each other—a divine presence within us and within everyone else. The first part of the secret of the ages is to come to realize that such a presence exists and responds to us. Jesus tells us that this presence is the presence of love, of life, and of peace.

But Jesus said more than this, and this is the second part of the great secret he unfolded for the ages. The Spirit is not only a presence; it is also a power. So we have two things to think about in discovering the secret of the ages. One is the divine presence, and the other is the divine power, and the divine power is a law of good that is available for any and every good purpose.

Jesus communed with this divine presence, and he definitely used this divine power. He plainly taught that we must first become acquainted with the presence, and then the power will be delivered to us. He said if you know God, you will not only find an intimate companionship, you will also discover a limitless power. The coming to understand this presence and this power is what Jesus called *knowing the truth* when he said, "And you will know the truth, and the truth will make you free."

Here is the secret of secrets, because Jesus implied that there is something that we can find out about and know, the very knowing of which produces freedom, happiness, health, harmony, success, and a right relationship with each other. Surely this is the secret of the ages, because it tells us about a power greater than we all are, a power that is so close to us that it is actually within us, a power that can be used for definite purposes.

So we come to the unfolding of the way this power that is greater than we are works through us and for us, and we will be amazed at its simplicity. Jesus said the power works through you when you have faith in it. Our faith in divine power is what gives us the ability to use it. This is why Jesus said, "Your faith has made you whole," "According to your faith be it done unto you," and again, "It is done unto you as you believe."

This is the secret of the power of Jesus that has been overlooked. It didn't seem possible that you and I could possess the knowledge of a power that, acting through our faith, can actually produce definite results in our personal experience and in the experience of those whom we wish to help.

Jesus taught what the right use of this power is. He said that there is a power you can use if you have faith in it, but he also said that this power is good, it is love, and being good and being love, it delivers itself to you only when you use it in love and for good purposes. These good purposes seem to mean everything that makes life worthwhile. Jesus used the power for healing the sick. As a matter of fact, he used it in the most commonplace things of life.

We need not be concerned as to whether or not divine power is given to us to use only occasionally or for some purposes. It can be used for any purpose that is constructive. There is a power for good in the universe greater than you are, and you can use it. Here we must be careful to remember that we are not that power, but we can use it. Just as we are not electrical energy, but we do use it to light our buildings and for many other purposes. If we felt that we were that power, then we should be sitting around trying to make things happen through our human will, and probably all we would get out of it would be a headache.

Jesus gives us specific instruction in his great teaching about prayer and faith. He disclosed the inner secret of prayer and faith, the thing that really makes it work, when he said that when you pray, believe that God has already made the gift, and God will make it. This means that the power greater than we are acts on our faith and tends to bring into our experience what we mentally accept.

You are surrounded by a creative power that acts on your thought the way you think it. This is the deep secret, the secret of the ages. It is a key to the understanding of how it is that prayers have been answered. We all know that certain prayers are answered and it seems as though others are not. No doubt every prayer is answered when the prayer is right, when it complies with three definite conditions that Jesus laid down.

The first condition is that we realize the divine presence. The next condition is that we believe in the greater power. And the third, that we use it for definite purposes through praying affirmatively, that is, through the prayer of acceptance.

Let's suppose we wish to use this power to bring a happier experience into our lives. Perhaps we wish for friends. Since the power already exists and is around as well as within us, and since faith is a certain way of thinking, we will have to begin with our thoughts, and we must watch ourselves very carefully to see whether or not we are affirming or denying our good. We will have to make our whole life a prayer of affirmation, a prayer of faith, and since even so exalted a thing as faith is a certain way of thinking, we should begin by saying to ourselves, "I have faith, and I have faith in faith. I do believe that God is present everywhere. I do believe that good is present everywhere. I do believe that the doorway of opportunity is open before me. I do believe that I am divinely guided. I do believe that the Spirit goes before me and prepares the way. I do believe that the good in my life is increasing. I do believe that every day I am meeting new circumstances and new situations. I do believe that divine love is bringing new friends to me. I do believe that health, happiness, and success belong to me."

If you want to prove to someone else that they can be happier and live a fuller life, first prove that you are happier and that you are living a fuller life. Everyone will believe what is proven, and everyone can prove what they believe if they believe it rightly. When Jesus said, "These signs will follow them that believe," he was sharing with us the secret of the ages.

He was definitely saying that we are surrounded by a power that reacts to us as we think. He was giving us the answer to the hope, the longing, and yearning of the ages, the questions that everyone asks: Does life make sense? What is it all about? Where do we go from here? Is anything worthwhile? And out of all this doubt and skepticism, out of all this discouragement, uncertainty, and fear, the voice of one who knew what he was talking about speaks directly to you and me, telling us that there is a power greater than we are that we can use. The power was always given, but only those who believe use it. So it looks as though even the power greater than we are is waiting our simple acceptance of it.

Does this seem too good to be true? Does this seem too wonderful to accept? Does this seem too profound to understand? Not at all. It is its very simplicity that eludes us. It is the directness of our approach to it that we have failed to understand. And now, more than anything else on Earth, the world needs the evidence of such divine power operating in human affairs. You and I cannot wait for some great teacher, some sublime genius, some awe-inspiring figure to appear. You and I are not waiting for such events. We are really waiting for our own acceptance.

All will have to begin with themselves. What do you and I believe about God? What do you and I think about the power greater than we are and its availability? Are we carefully guarding our thoughts? Are we trying to feel the divine presence in everything? Are we feeling out toward everything with love, and are we looking to God in faith?

We already possess the secret of the ages, but we haven't known we had it. Perhaps we are already using it but in the wrong way. Perhaps the realm of God is at hand but we haven't recognized it. Perhaps God's hand is in ours but we have failed to recognize the gentle pressure of its love. Let's share this secret with each other as the most glorious thing we possess, and let's use it for ourselves and for each other, because it is the gift of God to you and to me and to the whole world.

YOUR CREATOR'S HOUSE

Jesus was the greatest spiritual genius who ever lived. His whole teaching was given to show the intimate relationship we have with This Thing Called Life, with a power greater than we are, and with a law of good available to everyone, wherever we may be.

Jesus taught no long methods in our approach to God. He plainly taught that there is nothing between you and me and life. He taught that everyone is divine in their own right because God made them this way, and he told us that we should have a childlike approach to the Spirit, that there need be no formality in our coming to God. The approach is simple and direct—a spontaneous act of trust and faith.

In all his wonderful parables, he was telling us what this direct relationship to God is. Today we are going to talk about the best known of the parables of Jesus, the story of the prodigal son. It is the story of each one of us, because we all have left our parent's house and wandered into a far country.

Jesus begins this famous parable by telling the story of a father who had two sons. It seems that the younger of the sons asked for his portion of the family estate, because he wanted to be completely independent of his father. The father did not argue with his son or ask him what he was going to do, but divided his portion to him.

The young man, who now felt free to do as he pleased, took the money his father gave him and went into a far country. This "far country" represents a state of separation from the source of life. We travel into this far country when we separate ourselves from Spirit and try to go entirely on our own, as though we were isolated beings.

The young man soon wasted his substance in riotous living, but when he had spent everything, "a great famine arose in that land," and he found himself in want. A famine always arises when we separate ourselves from daily communion with the Spirit. It is then that we begin to be in want. The waters of our individual lives soon dry up when we separate ourselves from the well-spring of all being.

Having exhausted his resources, the prodigal son was compelled to sell his services to a citizen of the far country into which he had traveled, and soon he was sent into the field to feed swine. Perhaps Jesus used this comparison to show what a complete state of destitution the once well-cared for young man had fallen into. Jesus was talking to those who held the meat of swine to be unholy. Therefore, he was placing the plight of the young man in the worst possible light, that he had fallen to such low estate that he was a complete social outcast.

But the great teacher paints an even more dreary picture, because he said that the young man became so famished that he would gladly have eaten the husks that the swine were fed. "But no one gave unto him." Others may give us temporary food, clothing, and shelter, but life alone can give life. This is the meaning of the words, "No one gave unto him."

And now a remarkable thing happened to the young man. "He came to himself." This is one of the most important parts of the story. No matter how isolated from the source of life we seem to be, there is always something within us that can come to itself. Always, there is a pool of Spirit into which we may plunge. But first, we must remember who we are. We must find our divine center.

When he "came to himself," the young man remembered that in his father's house there had always been bread to eat. There had been servants. There had been luxury. There had been the fruit of the vine and the warmth of home. Remembering, hope sprang up within him, and he resolved to return to his father's house.

But, as with all of us, he had a deep sense of guilt because of what he had done. He said to himself that when he met his father, he would throw himself in the dust before him, confess his shame, and ask to be forgiven, without hoping actually to be reinstated. He would ask that he become as a servant in the house. At least this would give him protection, food, and shelter. He would be humble and meek, because he knew himself to be so unworthy.

Everyone makes this confession to themselves. Everyone resolves to return to the parent's house, and though we may feel unworthy, there is always an inward sense that somehow everything can be made right if we can only get back to the parent. There is a voice within that has never ceased speaking to us, a presence that has never ceased beckoning to us, a power greater than we are that has willed that we make this return journey.

So the young man started on his homeward journey, filled with both hope and despair, walking down the lonely road with tearful and downcast eyes, yet with a conviction stronger than his fears. Unless our faith was greater than our fears, none of us could make this return journey.

While the young man was yet far off, the father saw him and ran out to meet him and kissed him. This is one of the most glorious parts of the whole story, because it teaches us that God turns to us as we turn to God. We have only to make the choice, and the divine presence draws close to us, embracing us in its perfect love and wisdom.

The young man threw himself down before his father, saying that he was no more worthy to be called his child. This confession was good for him, as it is good for all of us. It is a purging of the soul and the mind by some inward fire that burns out the accumulated experiences of all our misspent time of folly.

Again, Jesus tells us of our true relationship with God. He tells us that the father did not argue with the son. He did not condemn him. He did not tell him he had to go through several years of penance in order to be restored. He did not ask where he had been or what he had been doing. He did not say, "You are unworthy to be my child." Rather, he told the servants to bring the best robe for him, a ring for his hand and shoes for his feet. He told them to prepare a feast, that they might rejoice because his child who was dead was alive again, because that which was lost had been found.

Divine givingness always implies an equal divine forgivingness. That which gives all asks only that we return the gift to the giver, and, behold, when this is done, the feast is already spread and the divine banquet has begun.

The young man, in ignorance, had departed from his father's house. Under divine guidance, he had returned. The father was there, the house was there, the servants were there, and the law of good was ready to serve him. The table was spread, the banquet was prepared, and the feast that had been interrupted by his departure continued.

Now we come to another part of this remarkable story. It is about the elder son, who was working in the fields when his young brother returned. Hearing music, he called one of the servants and asked what was the occasion for such merry-making. When he was told that his brother had returned and a feast had been prepared for him, he became angry and would not go in to the feast.

This elder son had an attitude of self-righteous bigotry that we all recognize in ourselves. He had been living in his father's house all the time, but he was living there from a sense of stern duty. The spontaneous joy of living had never flooded his life with warmth and color. He was good, but in a negative way. Jesus demands that we be good in a positive way. He said that he had come that we might have more abundant life, that his peace and joy might enter into us, and that the certainty of the love of God might bring to each the divine assurance of peace and security.

Just as the father did not argue with the younger son when he went into the far country, so he did not argue with the elder son who remained at home. When the elder son complained, the father said to him, "Son, you are always with me, and all that I have is yours." It was as though the father said to him, "My dear boy, why didn't you make merry with your friends? Why haven't you enjoyed the home in which you have been living? Surely," he says to the elder son, "you would not cast out your younger brother who has returned to his home. Come in and make merry with us. Forgive and forget." This was not a rebuke to the elder son; it was an explanation of his true relationship with the father.

Each of us is a combination of these two children. We refuse to enter into the parent's house, and we will not allow others to enter. But our sin is more largely of ignorance than of intent. Just as the younger son did not know that he must soon spend his substance, since all he could carry with him would be so limited, so the elder son did not realize that he had substance to spend. One traveled into a far country to discover his error; the other remained at home and failed to discover his mistake.

You and I represent each of these children combined in one. We have traveled into a far country and discovered that we could not live without God, and we have remained at home, sincerely believing that we belong to the divine family, but not having entered into the joys of our inheritance. We may as well forget all of our past mistakes and confusions. We have decided to return from the far country and live at home in joy. We have decided to enter into our divine inheritance here and now and to try to live as though we actually were children of the Most High, as though God were the host in the household of heaven to which we all belong.

How wonderful is this concept! How beautiful are the thoughts that come with it. The long years of waiting, periods of doubt and fear and uncertainty, have passed into oblivion as the sun of hope rises clear and bright across our pathway. Let us follow its rays until we discover that they lead to the sanctuary of the heart, the secret place of the Most High within us, where God and good reign supreme.

TEN STEPS IN
PERSONAL ACHIEVEMENT

I want us to build a ladder of personal achievement with ten steps in it, steps that I believe will help us to live happily and successfully and, in so doing, help us to help others in the glorious game of living.

Let's start with step number one: How to overcome negative mental attitudes. Our basic thought here should be: You can if you know you can. Negative thoughts will produce negative results, while positive thinking surrounds you with an atmosphere that tends to draw good into your experience. Successful people do not permit themselves to think of failure. They occupy their minds with positive thinking.

This doesn't mean arbitrary or dogmatic thinking. Rather, it means a sort of good-natured flexibility with yourself, because you are the greatest single asset you will ever possess. Practice thinking affirmatively and hopefully about everything you do, and let this include everything—your health, your happiness, and your success. Have a bright, happy, and cheerful outlook on life.

Feed your mind with nourishing thoughts just as you feed your body with nourishing food. Feed your mind with faith, hope, and enthusiastic expectancy. Replace every doubt with a faith stronger than the doubt. This is the first step in our ladder.

The second step should be to learn how to stop worrying. Worry is an acquired habit. You didn't worry when you were a child. Worry is the greatest energy waster we have. It not only depresses the mind, it depresses the physical system as well. It actually contests and retards circulation.

If you study the worry habit, you will find that you are either worrying about the past, the outlook for the future, or the things that are happening today. Worrying about the past will not help anyone. We should never look backward except to learn from experience. We do learn from experience, but we do not have to carry negative experiences along with us.

Each day say to yourself, "The past is gone, and I need no longer carry it along with me." Loose it and let it go, and look forward to the future with hope. Build up a great idea of yourself the way you would like to be, and work toward it, knowing that This Thing Called Life is your partner, God is your friend, and life wills you to be happy. Think, live, and feel this.

Our third step deals with overcoming any sense of inferiority you may have in your life. To begin with, realize that life has made you a little different from anyone else. You do not have to imitate. While you can and should learn from others, you can never be anyone but yourself, and no one can be you for you. Take this thought: "If God be for me, who can be against me."

Do not be afraid to look yourself squarely in the face. Do not be afraid to analyze your negative thoughts, so that for of every denial of your good, you can affirm the opposite. This thing we hear so much about called the inferiority complex is, after all, only a mental outlook on life. It is merely a denial that there is a power greater than you are, a power great enough to overcome every obstacle.

In our fourth step, let us think a little about your personality. It is through your personality that all outside contacts are made. Who are you? Where did you come from? You didn't create yourself. Your personality has its roots in a divinity within you, in God who is present everywhere, and since life has made you just a little different from all others, you need never be ashamed of yourself.

We always admire capable people, but the ones we really love are those who bring joy and happiness into our lives. Lovable personalities mean more to us than just people of great personal achievement. One we admire and the other we love, and it is better to be loved than it is to be admired.

This makes the whole thing rather simple. Love others, and they will love you. You never have to impress people. If your attitude toward others is one of friendship, your personality will take care of itself.

For the fifth step, let us next consider you and your everyday activities—what you are doing and how you are doing it. You must learn to make your work easy. The one who works the easiest accomplishes the most. This doesn't mean that you are not to put the best you have into your work. It means that you can let the burden drop out of it.

You are not carrying the world around on your shoulders. It is sustained by a power greater than you are, and the game of living isn't intended to be a sad, heavy, dreary affair. "Easy does it." When the strain is taken out of what you are doing, you can do three times as much without any sense of fatigue. You will generally find that it is mostly yourself, and not your work, that needs to be changed.

When you get up in the morning, don't think of the many things you have to do today, but rather, "I am doing this thing, this one thing, and doing it with joy." This will really produce efficiency. Here, as everywhere else, know that you are in silent partnership with life. Try to feel that you meet God in the office, in the home, on the street, in people, everywhere. Somehow or other, as you meet God in people and in things, God seems to meet you.

Our sixth step is to learn to count your blessings. Did you ever make an inventory of the good things in your life and write down how much you have to be thankful for? Are you glad that you are alive, glad that you have a family and friends, glad that you have the opportunity to express yourself, glad that there is a great certainty coming into your life, a feeling that you belong to the universe in which you live? When you count your blessings, don't omit the little ones. Counting your blessings will help you more than most anything else you could possibly do.

In step number seven, we learn how necessary it is to forgive both ourselves and others. The great teacher said, "Forgive, and you will be forgiven." You cannot be a radiant personality if you hold grudges or resentments in your mind.

In taking this step of forgivingness, remember that you cannot practice this attitude with lip service alone. It must be a thing of the heart. Let us learn to say, with James Whitcomb Riley, "O, thou who doest all things, help us who see with mortal eyes to overlook the rest." We have to create one great blanket of forgivingness that can be summed up only in the word *love*, and love alone is best.

Now we come to our seventh step—getting along with others. Only mentally sick people become hermits. If we don't get along with others, it is because we are afraid of them and because we believe they can in some way rob us of our own security. But getting along with others doesn't mean that we always agree with them. It means that such disagreements as we have are not harsh or unkind.

How can you get along with others unless you first learn to get along with yourself? If you have been too critical of yourself, take a piece of paper and write down everything about yourself you think is admirable, and don't forget to put down your hopes and longings, because they are prophetic of what you may become. As you think of others, think of the things that are admirable about them, and when you talk of them, these are the things you should talk about. People like to be appreciated.

This is more than a Pollyannaish attitude. This is an ability that great and rare people possess. It is the ability you will always find in those who are surrounded by many friends, and it is as simple as this: See the good in yourself and in others, and build on this. Expect everyone to be friendly, and you will lose all self-consciousness in meeting people. There is really no great and no small. We are all just human beings trying to get along together.

Let us take prayer and affirmative meditation for our ninth step in personal achievement. Prayer is not something that should be reserved for the emergencies of life alone. Our whole lives should be a prayer. Prayer is both a skill and an art, and in a certain sense it is the mental mechanism through which spiritual power flows into our everyday living. Prayer hooks up the dynamo of the mind with a power greater than we are. It is our line of communion with it.

Prayer should be affirmative. Get out your New Testament and read again all the prayers of Jesus. You will be amazed at how affirmative they are. They are like great recognitions of God's goodness, of life's abundance, of the peace, the poise, the power, and love that are at the center of everything.

Now we come to the concluding step in this ladder—how to get the most out of your religion. I have no way of knowing what your religion may be, but I am sure that you have one, and I know it is good. The question is not whether you or I have a religion. It is, are we using it? Are we getting the most out of it?

If you want to get the most out of your religion, you will have to share it with others. When people are gathered together in prayer and meditation, a great field of faith is created that multiplies the faith of each individual member and that can react on all who are gathered together. There is only one institution in the world where you can find this gathering together and unity of faith, and that is the institution of the church.

Our ladder is pretty complete by now, but, like all ladders, it is no good unless we climb, unless we use it to go from where we are to where we would like to be. We have put together a ladder of hope, of faith, of expectancy, something that joins us with the invisible and with each other. Let us be sure that we climb it, rung by rung, because this is the ladder that joins heaven with earth.

FAITH MEANS FREEDOM

When Jesus said, "It is done unto you as you believe," he not only announced a law of faith, but he explained how it works. If there is a law of faith, it is right where you are, and it will operate like any other law in nature. For instance, it will work like the law of gravitation, which automatically holds everything in place. But as far as you are concerned, it will hold personal things where you place them. You cannot change the law of gravitation; you can only change your position in it. As you shift objects around in the position that seems desirable to you, gravity will hold them there.

Suppose you want to change the position of the furniture in your room. You move the piano from one place to another. This is an act of choice on your part. Perhaps you wish to move the stove into the living room. This might seem an eccentric act, but the law does not question it. It automatically holds things where you place them. It operates on your decision. Jesus proclaimed a law of faith that acts on your belief in like manner. Not only is there a law that does something for you, but in doing so, it is limited to your belief. This is the important thing to remember.

It is only common sense to recognize that what this law does for you, it must of necessity do *through* you. The gift of life is not complete until it is accepted. If you believe only in a little good, then the law will be compelled to operate on that little good. The law itself knows nothing about big and little any more than the law of gravitation would know that a mountain is heavier than a marble. It automatically holds everything in place. And the power that does this is invisible, as are all forces in nature.

Now, shift this whole proposition over into the invisible law of good that acts on your faith. This law is like a mirror reflecting your mental attitudes. Therefore, if you say, "I can have a little good," it will produce this small amount of good for you. But if you say, "All the good there is is mine" with equal certainty, it will produce a larger good. If you believe that wherever you go, you will meet with love and friendship, with appreciation and gratitude, then this will become the law of your life.

Often, good and sincere people ask if it is right to use divine power for personal purposes. No one thinks it wrong to use other laws of nature for personal purposes. The laws of mind and spirit are natural laws. Do not hesitate to use these laws for any purpose that is constructive. It is no more selfish to use spiritual law for personal purposes than it is to plant a garden for your personal use. Moreover, there is no escaping this law, because it is as intimate as your own thought, as personal as your own being.

Use your intellect, imagination, and feeling for the purpose of seeing and sensing freedom instead of bondage, joy instead of unhappiness, plenty instead of want, health in place of disease. The very denial of your good keeps that good from you. Reversing this process through affirmation will bring about the good you desire.

It might come as a surprise to many, if when they say, "My aching head!" "My bad back!" or "My poor circulation!" you were to tell them they are actually using a creative law in a negative way. The laws of mind do not work in one instance while refusing to operate in another. Every time you think, you are using the law of mind. How careful, then, you should be to think constructively.

Mental laws are as real as physical laws, and the use of your creative power is as natural as the use of electricity, but there is not as much known about it. It is because the law of life is at the center of your being that your thought is creative. Your individual use of this law becomes the law of your individual being.

While this is one of the most profound concepts ever believed in, it is also one of the most simple. Instead of having an individual creative mind, you really have an individual or personal use of a law that is infinite. Through this law, you can bring things to you from the uttermost parts of the earth. The mind principle around you is reactive to your thought. Its chief characteristic is its susceptibility to impression. It receives the slightest vibration of thought and acts on it.

Since this law acts like a mirror, when you withdraw old images of thought and place new ones in front of this mirror of mind, the old reflections or conditions cease to exist and the new ones take their place. But if you only half withdraw the old images and only half create new ones, your experience will partake of the nature of both kinds of thought.

Jesus was very explicit in his teaching of the use of faith. He said that if you ask for bread, you will not receive a stone. This is equal to saying that if you plant a rose bush, it will not become a lemon tree. The law of faith operates with integrity on the definite idea, thought, expectancy, or acceptance implanted in it.

But the seed must be left in the creative soil of mind until it can mature. There is a time for sowing as well as a time for harvest. Plants must not be pulled up or interrupted in the process of their growth.

They must be watered with hope, fertilized with expectancy, and cultivated with enthusiasm, gratitude, and joyous recognition.

If the law operates automatically, then you do not coerce, concentrate, or compel it. You provide mental attitudes that it may operate on. You do not hold the law in place; you hold your ideas in place. This is your individual effort. This process is not so much a problem of will as it is one of willingness. The only important role the will plays is in a decision to keep your thought in place long enough to permit the law to operate. This is not a prayer of beseechment, but a recognition or acknowledgment of right action.

It will be well to consider the difference between outlining and choosing. As an individual, you have the right to choose. Being an individual, you cannot escape the necessity of choice. You do the choosing; the law of good does the outlining. This is the distinction between choice and outline. If you choose to plant a tomato seed, you have chosen a tomato plant, but you do not outline how many leaves will grow on the plant or how many stalks it will have. That belongs to God's law of cause and effect.

When you say, "I know that the divine intelligence is attracting certain conditions to me" and when you have affirmed your union with good, you can go about the business of everyday life with no sense of anxiety, knowing that the law of good is working for you. Faith is the most important thing in your life. It is impossible to conceive the grandeur of what it can do. The whole mental scope must be broadened and deepened, the whole expectancy must reach out to more, the whole imagination must lend its feeling to grateful acceptance and joyous recognition of the power greater than you are.

Life wishes to make the gift, because in doing so, it is flowing into its own self-expression. You might say that gravity wishes to hold an object in place because this is its nature. As a matter of fact, it cannot help doing so. But if you place the oven in the living room and keep it on during a hot summer day, you will be uncomfortable. If you place it too close to the draperies, no doubt they will catch fire.

This does not mean that the law would have any evil intent. You could as well put the oven in the garden. You might put an electric heater in your refrigerator and the ice would melt, not because the law wishes to destroy the contents of the refrigerator, but because laws are always impersonal. Jesus told his disciples that while there is a law of belief, and of necessity they must always be using it, being individuals with free will they must expect to reap as they have sown.

You wish to reap joy, happiness, love, friendship, health, harmony, and success. Could you expect to keep your mind filled with such thoughts for yourself unless it was filled with similar thoughts for others? Of course not. This would not make sense. Therefore, Jesus said to love your enemies, be kind to everyone, "give, and to you shall be given." Moreover, he said that when you give, the gift will return to you multiplied. What a marvelous concept this is! It seems too good to be true. Yet, plant a seed in the ground, and it multiplies its own type many times. You have a right to expect that what you wish for others will be returned to you through others. But you have no right to expect that you can reap where you have not sown.

The marvelous teaching of Jesus is not quite as soft as it sounds. His words are statements of the great law of cause and effect, the law that produces justice without judgment, the inevitable result of the law that works with mathematical certainty. You cannot love and hate at the same time, nor can anyone else. Therefore, this person of wisdom said that light overcomes darkness. He did not say that darkness overcomes light.

Disregarding the softness and beauty of the words of Jesus, the marvelous grandeur of them, you will always find this cold, hard fact staring you in the face. Jesus taught the operation of a law of cause and effect. He said that not one tiny bit of it can be changed. All the poetry, wit, knowledge, and art of the ages cannot alter the fact that love alone begets love. Peace alone attracts peace. Only that which goes forth in joy can return with gladness. Give, and to you will be given, good measure, pressed down and running over.

You need not force or coerce, but you must obey the law. If you can see God in everything, then God will look back at you through everything. This is the law of give and take. When the time comes that nothing goes forth from you other than that which you would be glad to have return, then you will have reached your heaven.

WHO IS YOUR WORST ENEMY?

One of the ancient sages of China said, "O human, having the power to live, why will you die?" These words were spoken thousands of years ago, but they might have been written yesterday by a modern physician or psychiatrist. "Having the power to live, why will you die?"

We sometimes wonder what is wrong with us and what is wrong with the whole world. We are told that eighty-five percent of our accidents are unconsciously invited, and that perhaps two-thirds of our physical ailments are caused by wrong emotional adjustments to life. Doctors and nurses are spending much of their time trying to put us together after we tear ourselves apart. This really isn't a reflection against our intelligence or desire to be well, happy, and successful. It is a comment on the way our minds work and the often fatal result of wrong thinking.

Some people believe that God causes us to suffer in order to see how much we can take. But you might as well say that God doesn't want us to have electric lights; that God wants us to use candles. This is too absurd to give serious thought to. We now accept that the laws of nature never change. They have always existed, and when we understand and know how to use them, they will serve us.

Many who are devoting their lives to the study of who or what is humankind's worst enemy are coming to believe that we ourselves are our own worst enemy, that This Thing Called Life could wish us no ill. Life seems to say that there is a right road, a good road to follow, and when you do follow it, all will be well. One of the big things of modern discovery is that we really are our own worst enemy and, perhaps from the standpoint of nature, our *only* enemy. These discoveries are so great as to startle the imagination. Among other things, they show that it is possible, through right mental and emotional adjustment to life, to get rid of a large part of our physical ailments.

We actually have a chart and a guide that shows us how to do this. But like all charts and guides, the directions must be followed if we hope for good results. You are more than a physical body and a physical environment. As the Bible states, you are a living soul. Life has endowed you with two great gifts: your intellect and will; and your emotion and feeling. And it is not possible to separate them.

You are a living soul, and you have a physical body and a physical environment. The relationship between body and environment is a thing of thought and feeling, so much so that it is difficult to tell where one begins and the other leaves off. So finely adjusted is the balance between mind and body that it is impossible for us to be well unless we are happy. It is equally impossible to live happily with others unless we know how to get along with them happily.

We are interested today in the relationship between your mind and your body. I recently read an article by one of our great spiritual leaders, Dr. Norman Vincent Peale, who is doing so much in helping people to become properly adjusted to life. He writes about a woman who practiced spiritual meditation. One day in meditation, she listened to her heartbeat until she became conscious of a certain persistent rhythm and regularity to it. There came to her a deep feeling that she was in rhythm with life, that she was one with life and one with God.

She next tried listening to the rustling of reeds, and she seemed to sense the same rhythm there, as though the rustling of the reeds in the wind was only another form of a universal rhythm. She next tried listening to the rhythm of ocean waves. Again, she seemed to enter into the same rhythm of life, as though there were one harmony running through everything.

This shouldn't seem strange, because there must be fundamental laws that govern everything, and these laws would have to be laws of harmony. No matter how much we are out of tune with nature, nature itself is never out of tune with us. Its rhythm keeps right on, and in a certain sense nature seems always to be saying to us, "Enter into my harmony. Become part of my rhythm, and all will be well." It is no different from the Bible saying, "Look unto me and be saved, all the ends of the earth," or where it says, "Be still, and know that I am God."

I recently read a story about a certain family who had a baby whose food didn't agree with it, and they were advised to feed the infant ground raw liver. This was successful, and the baby was getting along all right with the raw liver added to its diet. Its little stomach never seemed to revolt against it. But one day, they found that the child again did not retain its food.

In casting around for a reason, this is what they found. This particular day, the child was being cared for by its grandmother. It seems that grandmother revolted at the thought of feeding the child raw liver, yet with a stern sense of duty she complied with the wishes of the family, and here is the plot in this little drama. Grandmother was a stern and well-controlled soul. She would feed the child the liver all right, but emotionally she so revolted against it that the child regurgitated for her. The next day, when the mother gave the child the same diet, it was retained in complete harmony.

How little we realize the result of the thoughts and feelings of those around us or the result of our own thinking. We know that if we are agitated or irritated when we eat, our food will not digest properly. If we are strained and overwrought, it affects the digestive tract, and when we are worried and anxious, we do not rest well.

You and I are not psychiatrists, nor is it necessary that we understand the relationship between every emotion and our physical well being. Fortunately, hundreds of well trained people are doing this for us. There are plenty of good books on the subject available in every library today. It is not necessary that we become technical analysts to understand them. Moreover, they are very simple and finally add up to this: Our thoughts and feelings do affect our physical system, whether we like it or not. Therefore, be certain that your thoughts and feelings are in harmony with the rhythm of life. Cultivate calmness. Acquire a non-worry habit. Gain confidence in yourself and in the world in which you live.

But how can you do this if you feel that life is against you and that you are left alone to struggle as best you may against terrific odds? Here is where faith enters, because there can be no complete confidence and assurance in the personal self alone. You and I know that we do not govern the laws of nature. We either comply with them or operate against them. It seems as though we have been operating against them for a long time. The time has come when we must learn to comply with them. We have to sort of re-evaluate things and come into a new understanding of life.

In his wonderful book, *Lead Kindly Light*, Vincent Shean writes that he once asked Mahatma Gandhi what is the true meaning of renunciation. Gandhi's reply was that the true meaning of renunciation is that we renounce the world as it appears to be and permit God to give it back to us as it really is. Like Jesus, he had penetrated the true meaning of life and, in so doing, had discovered that it was not necessary at all to deny the physical world or to say that a tree isn't a tree or a cat isn't a cat or a house isn't a house or a physical body isn't a physical body.

It was not the reality of these things that Gandhi denied or renounced. What he renounced was the thought that these things are separated from God and life. Like the prophet of old, Gandhi knew that the earth is the Lord's and the fullness thereof. He knew that there is a rhythm of all life and that when we renounce the false rhythm, God will give us the true rhythm of all life.

The Old Testament states that our enemies will be those of our own household. This does not mean our spouses or children, or our grandparents or in-laws. It means ourselves. The Bible also says that those who control the members of their own household are greater than those who conqu a city. Here, the symbol of a city means something outside us, but the members of our own household are our thoughts and feelings.

You and I are our worst enemies—take it or leave it, like it or not, it is the simple truth. But this should come to us as tidings of great joy. It should come as glad news, because if we are our worst enemies, why couldn't we become our best friends? And how we all need a friend. In a certain sense, the first and best friend you will ever have will be yourself. Life has willed it this way, because no matter how close others may be to you and no matter how much you may love them or be loved by them, no one can live for you but yourself.

In the busy hours of the day and the long hours of the night, everyone lives much alone in their own thoughts. So let's become our own best friends and never withhold friendship from others. Let's learn to take ourselves for better or for worse, and, under the guidance of divine love, let's enter into a new faith in This Thing Called Life, in the power greater than we are.

Every organ, action, and function of the physical body and our whole being is rooted in pure Spirit. This is what Jesus meant when he said, "Be therefore perfect, even as your Creator which is in heaven is perfect." Jesus had already said that it is neither here nor there, neither in the mountain nor at Jerusalem, that you are to find your real heaven, but within yourself.

Plato, one of the greatest intellects of all time, said that there is a divine pattern of every organ of the body existing in pure Spirit, and one of his followers said that whenever any organ of the body gets out of rhythm with life, it begins to suffer pain, and its whole endeavor is to get back to its pattern that it may be healed. Jesus said, "Come unto me, all you that labor and are heavy laden, and I will give you rest."

I cannot help but believe that they were talking about the same thing, and I think they meant that we must unite ourselves with the Spirit within us, a Spirit that you and I did not create. We didn't put it there; we are merely discovering that it was there all the time.

We should begin to practice the presence of God within us in a very normal, natural, and spontaneous manner and with utmost simplicity. Everyone who has ever talked to the God within has had a direct answer. Let us see if we cannot learn to renounce our fears and our doubts, all this inward shaking and quaking and apprehension, and let God give us back to ourselves as we really are.

SPIRITUAL ARMAMENT

Leaders in this and in other countries have asked that we pray for peace in the world, because everyone realizes that we are in a period of great crisis—a crisis that many people feel can mark the beginning of a new and a united effort toward world peace.

The over-pessimistic are afraid that this crisis might lead to complete world devastation, but people with hope and faith should not feel this way. Rather, we should feel that this crisis can lead to something permanent and good, something that will make the world a better place in which to live, bringing individual and collective safety, personal liberty, and freedom and justice for all.

It is my belief that this is the greatest responsibility that ever came to one nation, and with it, the greatest opportunity that has come to our great country, which, united with other democracies, is making a united and, perhaps, a last effort to preserve those values that are dear to all freedom-loving people throughout the world. As we arm for this conflict, we have the inward assurance that right is on our side, and we should clear our minds of all confusion about this, because there is not and never has been any political or economic system that can equal democracy.

It is democracy that we are fighting for, a democracy that alone can give freedom to the world and make possible of realization the great hope of humanity. In this effort, we should all unite. There is no sacrifice too great to make for it, and, indeed, such sacrifices as we think we are called on to make should not be considered in the light of sacrifice at all but rather in the light of the opportunity that is placed before each one of us to join in this great aspiration.

Freedom is something that is won with difficulty and kept only through eternal vigilance. What does freedom really mean as it works out through the only instruments that can maintain its purpose—the instruments of government conceived in the idea that all people are equal before God? That each one of us is an individual in our own right, and that each of us should have the privilege of self-expression, provided our desires do not infringe on the rights of others.

Democracy is a great cooperative enterprise through which this is made possible. Since time began and throughout the ages, this has been the hope and the dream of humankind, first finding expression in the Magna Carta, where the right to rule was seized from despotic rulers, and coming full blossom in the Declaration of Independence and the Constitution, undoubtedly the two greatest human documents ever written.

These instruments conceived the faith of great and wise and good people, people who were not only good Americans, great enough to give birth to our country, but also great historians, people like Jefferson and Adams and Franklin and Washington. These were people of great intellect, great souls, and great faith. That which they conceived has borne the fruit of human liberty as no other system ever did.

It would be a wonderful thing if we should all reread the Declaration of Independence and the Constitution of the United States and try to think out their meaning, line by line and word by word. Here we find not only the supreme ideal in government, but the definite and specific directions for working it out, and it is simple enough—a federal union so organized that it may protect the interests of the common good without infringing on the rights of the individual citizen.

Our ancestors were wise indeed when they worked out a system that bound all together in one common purpose without overlooking the fact that each person is an individual, that every state and each political subdivision down to the precinct in which you and I live should be able to preserve the identity and the integrity of all groups, from the largest to the smallest.

In doing this, those who wrote these two great documents surely did so under divine guidance. All you have to do is to look around in nature and you find that while everything comes from one nature, everything bears the stamp of a unique individuality. The great lesson life is trying to teach us is that we are all rooted in God but each person is an individualized center in the divine being. We have what Emerson called "unity at the center and variety at the circumference." But unity does not mean uniformity. Unity means a oneness of purpose. Unity means what is best and safe for the majority without losing sight of each member of that majority and each location in it. So we have a federal government, a United States, within which union we have States' rights and counties and townships and municipalities, right down to the smallest unit, each free from the tyranny of the other, and we have checks and balances, so that no one group at the top can dictate the policies of the lesser groups down the scale of our political system.

This is the system on which our country has grown and prospered. No doubt there are many defects in it, because after all we are all human beings. But it is infinitely stronger than it is weak, and on its preservation rests the hope of the world.

Amidst the present day confusion, we should not lose sight of another great and wonderful thing that is happening. For the first time in the history of the world, democracies everywhere are uniting against aggression. Fifty-two out of fifty-nine nations have made a solemn pledge to uphold the hands of freedom, to protect the idea of liberty, and to do their utmost not only to preserve the freedom that they now have but to safeguard it for all time.

We must not lose faith in the purpose of the United Nations, because it, too, is going through the first pangs of a new birth, the travail of bringing about that which it has conceived, which is really a continuation and expansion of the very idea conceived in the minds of our ancestors. There will always be great nations and small nations, just as in our country we have some States larger than others.

We are now seeing the necessity of a world law, to the mainte-nance of which all nations, great or small, will contribute the best they have—that the strong will protect the weak without overpowering them, that the great will live with the small without subduing them, that cooperation will take the place of aggression, that government will rule without tyranny through the common consent of the gov-erned, and that individual freedom will unfurl its flag of liberty on the ramparts of a world union whose motto will still read, "Of the people, by the people, and for the people," and whose united strength will guarantee that such a united people will not perish from the face of the earth.

Democracy is a spiritual idea, and it must and will be preserved. But democracy is exactly what Abraham Lincoln said—"Of the peo-ple, by the people, and for the people"—and you and I are the people. Therefore, each has an important role to play. A duty is imposed on all of us to take our part, each in our small way, toward the keeping and guarding of that freedom, without which life could have no meaning to any of us.

That which was born in faith must be kept through faith. As never before, our thoughts, our meditations, our hopes, and our prayers must rise in one common accord, and you and I should form the habit of taking definite time each day to pray for peace with justice, because there is no peace possible without it. We should take time each day to pray, to know, and to meditate on the thought, and to meditate affirmatively with complete acceptance that our leaders everywhere are being guided by the all-sustaining wisdom and upheld by the all-sustaining power of good, and we should pray for the peace of our own minds, that we will not become confused.

But faith without works is dead. We should not only pray, we should act, each contributing the best they have to the common purpose, each willing to make any sacrifice necessary, not a sacrifice reluctantly made, but as one who offers all that one has to give for two great purposes. The first is, in a certain sense, a selfish one, because we all desire self-preservation, but the second, in the greater sense that there can be no individual self-preservation without the preservation of all.

In doing this, we must be wise, not shutting our eyes to the fact that there is much propaganda against this idea of liberty. It is the duty of each one to report such propaganda to the proper authorities, because, after all, it is your liberty and my liberty that is to be preserved. It is unthinkable that our soldiers should be on the front line of sacrifice only to discover that misplaced freedom in the name of liberty is attacking them from the rear. There must be no fifth, sixth, or seventh column in our ranks, because liberty must put up a united front. It would be a poor general who, in advancing against the foe, would fail to protect the ranks in the rear.

Our soldiers are at the front, and they have a right to ask that the other hundred and fifty million of us at the rear will protect that for which they are fighting. This is your business and it is my business, and we should take it seriously, and we should take it with deep conviction and with a complete faith in that power greater than we are, in God, a faith exercised in the long hours of the night and acted on in every hour of the day.

If the whole nation works together and prays together, a great moral and spiritual power—an actual soul force—will penetrate the whole world, helping to bring confidence and calm judgment and right action until the crisis will have passed. Freedom need never be ashamed of itself, nor liberty bow to despair. God is always on the side of right, and faith will always conquer fear.

We cannot doubt but that the great mass of humanity in every nation must desire peace, and our country is trying to inform those behind the Iron Curtain that we have no ill will toward them as citizens. We wish to bring them peace and justice, and in our prayers we should know that this idea is being received and accepted. I believe there is a silent communion of mind with mind and that all of us have ample enough evidence of this fact in our everyday lives.

Thoughts and ideas are contagious, as we have so well learned in the last years of false propaganda. Why shouldn't there be a true propaganda, a spiritual propaganda? If your thoughts and mine reach each other's, as they most certainly do, why shouldn't our united thoughts penetrate every location on earth with a feeling of goodwill to the humble citizens of every country? I am sure they can.

Yes, the world is possibly at the point of the greatest crisis in all human history, and there seem to be two attitudes we can assume. One is calmness, faith, and conviction; the other, world despair, and despair is unthinkable. Let's then, each in our own way, dedicate our time, our service, our hope, and our spiritual conviction to the common cause of liberty and justice for all, and let's work without tiring and pray without ceasing. We know that on the battlefront and in the rear guard something alive with meaning is taking place, something vibrant with hope is happening, something latent with the possibility of the future is being conceived.

The destiny of the world is at stake, and this includes your world and my world. The world cannot exist half slave and half free. The decision is being made now. These are indeed times that try our souls, but it is written that "they that dwell in the secret place of the Most High will abide under the shadow of the Almighty." Let's pray that our soldiers abide under that shadow and that all the invisible forces of good go with them, even as does our love and gratitude.

Put God to Work
in Your Experience

I want to tell you about a friend whose business was failing. My friend and his partners had tried everything they could think of without success, and so they decide they would have to go through bankruptcy. But I knew my friend believed in prayer and faith. Just before they decided everything was lost, he asked his partners to wait a week before they came to a final decision.

He went home and stayed by himself for a whole week, trying to make his mind receptive to divine guidance, and he asked that God would give him whatever ideas were necessary to re-establish himself. He kept himself in a receptive mood with this one thought in mind: "Divine intelligence within me knows what to do." He kept his mind in a prayerful and an expectant attitude.

During this week when he was alone, an idea came to him that he felt could be applied to his business. So he brought this idea to his partners, whose first reaction was that it was perfectly ridiculous. It couldn't be done. No one had ever done it that way, and it wouldn't work. "But," he said to them, "we are up against it. We have tried everything else.

We are on the brink of failure. We really haven't anything to lose."

So they decided that since they had nothing to lose, there was no reason why they shouldn't try any idea. The thoughts that had come to him in his meditation were so clear and so definite that they were like a chart that they could follow. They were like instructions that could be carried out. So they applied these ideas to their business, and in a few months the firm was again on a sound footing. They were prosperous and expanding. It became the habit of all of them to gather together for meditation for the direct purpose of receiving divine guidance in their everyday affairs.

This man was so impressed by what happened, he was so moved by it, that he decided to withdraw from business and spend the rest of his life as a spiritual counselor for people who were trying to solve practical problems of everyday business life. He called this "God In Business."

This is a very simple story of the practical application of divine guidance in everyday life. The lesson we should learn from it is that we all have access to the power and the intelligence of This Thing Called Life. There is a place in your mind where you merge with the Divine. There is a secret place of the Most High within everyone, and we should seek to discover this secret place. There is a power greater than we are, and we should learn how to use it.

Why shouldn't we think of business as an activity of divine intelligence, since the exchange of thoughts and ideas and commodities is necessary in human affairs? Why shouldn't you feel that you have a silent partner, that you can receive inspiration and guidance from the supreme intelligence?

What did my friend really do? You and I want to use his experience as a lesson in our own affairs. First of all, he got still within himself and said, "There is a power greater than I am. The mind of God is present everywhere, and it is guiding me into right action. It is doing this today."

In California, we depend much on our water supply. We are always glad when the rainy season comes, and we know that nature is storing a water reserve in the mountain tops, blanketing them with snow, held in reserve so that when the proper time comes, it may irrigate our lands. God—This Thing Called Life—causes the snow to fall on the mountain tops, and then, in due season, the warmth of the sun melts this snow and, by an automatic process of gravitation, causes the water to flow down into the valleys so that we may direct it into our irrigation ditches and spread it out over the land.

Life gives us the tools; we have to use them. But it is from the high mountain tops that we receive the inspiration to act. "I will lift up my eyes unto the hills, from whence comes my help. My help comes from the Lord, which made heaven and earth." God has provided a mountain top in everyone's mind. We are all receiving power from on high. Life comes from an invisible source that flows down through us from a power greater than we are.

We must keep the channel clear. We must provide a way through which the water of Spirit may flow down into our minds and out into action in everyday living. How can we do this unless we believe that there is such a mountain top, that the rain and snow do come from heaven, and that the warmth of the sun does melt the snow, and, what is perhaps more important than anything else, that the water flows from a higher to a lower level by a law of its own, as though we were acted upon by a higher power, which we most certainly are, or may be if we give our consent.

We must give our consent. This is where faith comes in, faith in a power greater than we are, and an equal faith that this power flows through even the commonplace, the everyday things of life. God's law is not reserved for emergencies only. We should always be led of the Spirit.

This means that we should pray without ceasing. We should keep the mind open at all times, ready to receive impressions, because we are surrounded by a divine intelligence that flows around us and through us.

How should we proceed in drawing on this intelligence in everything we do? First, we must believe that such an intelligence exists. Then we must make our minds a channel through which it can flow, because there is no use catching inspiration from on high unless we actually bring it down into what we are doing.

A business is a distributing point for thoughts, ideas, and commodities. It is a place where those things are gathered together and then sent out along the routes of trade and commerce. We couldn't get along without business activities, and we shouldn't think of them as something common or material or unspiritual. We should think of business as one of the activities of the Divine Mind, and we should think of "God In Business" in the most natural manner.

We are too apt to think of spiritual things as something reserved only for the salvation of the soul, but this was not the attitude that Jesus took. While he said that we should seek God first, he also said that all these other things will be added to our faith, and "all these other things" means whatever we are doing that is good and constructive—whatever we are doing, whenever we are doing it, and wherever we are doing it.

One part of the mind is already on that mountain top we are talking about, because there is a place in you and in me that lives above confusion and fear, and no matter how disturbed our thought may be, if we get quiet long enough and listen deeply enough, we will receive some thought, some idea which, carried into action, can lead to success.

When we want to learn a new trade or a new profession, we expect to give some time to studying it, and we expect to be rewarded as a result of the time spent. It is just the same in developing the ability to cooperate with the silent partner, the power greater than we are, in our business affairs.

The happy thing about this is that we don't have to attend any university or trade school. We don't have to go anywhere. The instruction we need comes from within, and what we are listening to is not a teacher who is delivering a lecture from a platform, but the teacher of teachers, the divine intelligence that is already within us, and the place we go is inside ourselves.

We will have to spend time receiving the instruction. This is what is meant by prayer and meditation. Prayer means getting still inside your own mind and communing with the invisible, and the most effective prayer is that of affirmation, which means that we accept the answer even though we do not as yet see its results.

I have known many successful business people who have practiced this over a period of years, and the results are so definite that no one could doubt their reality. I have seen it in every type of profession. I have seen it in manufacturing plants, on the stage and screen. I have seen it in creative writing and in every form of art, and I have never yet known it to fail.

I believe in "God In Business," and I believe in the business of human living.

Whether you are running a store or shop or writing a poem, there is always something greater than you that you can call on. There is always more energy than you have ever used, more creative thoughts than you have ever known, more vitality than you have ever drawn on. There is a plot for everyone's play, an idea for everyone's written or spoken word, a better way to run anyone's business. There is always an inspiration for anyone who will listen for it.

Think of "God In Business" not as a vague idea or an idle dream, but as something dynamic and practical. And if things aren't going just right, see what you can do to bring about a better condition. It is certain that Jesus told his disciples where to fish when he said, "Cast your nets on the other side." It is certain that he found money in the fish's mouth to pay the tax, and when the disciples were hungry, Jesus fed them. Jesus was a practical idealist. He knew how to apply divine power to everyday problems.

The thing that has always impressed me about the life of Jesus, and impresses me more now than ever before, is that he never seemed to feel that one vocation or calling was higher or lower than another. He knew that all the good activities we engage in are necessary while we are in this world, and so he always said that we should hook them up with the power greater than we are.

Whatever the human need was, he always said to ask God about it and God will tell you the answer. But he said that when you ask God, believe that God is actually going to do it.

Let us take this great example, then, as something to follow, and not as a myth or a fable. Since it is our own minds and not something outside us that have to come into agreement and exercise the faith and conviction necessary to this silent partnership, we must train our minds to believe, and we should take time every day to do this, affirming that God is bringing new ideas to us, that the universe is chock full of ideas, that they are flowing into our own minds every moment and out into action through us.

I don't care how confused or upset or discouraged you may think you are, or what the situation that surrounds you may appear to be, or how disastrous the outlook, because if you know that with God all things are possible, if you know that you actually are in partnership with God, and if you learn to feel the presence of this power greater than you are and accept the guidance of this mind that knows everything, and if you keep a place open in your own mind, always up there on the mountain top, you will find that power will begin to flow down into your affairs.

You will find that you begin to do things in a new and better way. There will come a hope, an expectancy, a new power and vitality that will give a new direction to all you think, and this will be followed by action, even in the most commonplace things of life. So let's put a sign over the doorway of our establishment that reads "God In Business" and see to it that we never take it down.

Put Your
Best Self Forward

Shakespeare said, "There is nothing good or bad but thinking makes it so." Whether or not this immortal bard was one hundred percent right in this, one thing is certain: The mind does play some very weird tricks on us, some of them so startling as to almost convince us that we are actually obsessed.

I once worked with a woman for several months who almost continually heard voices, or thought she did, and this is not at all an uncommon experience. These voices seemed to keep her awake at night. She was so obsessed with the idea of obsession that for sometime it was impossible even to convince her that she was really holding a conversation with her own mind.

Finally, one evening while I was working for her, it came to me so clearly that there is only one mind in the universe, and this mind cannot be obsessed, and she represented this mind, since God is all there is. The next day, I called on her and was met at the door by a person who was completely transformed. She greeted me with the words, "I'm all right." Naturally, I asked her just what had happened, and she said, "Sometime during the night, it came to me that my whole trouble was with myself, that I have actually been controlled by thoughts that I now know were my own."

This mind of ours is a funny thing, isn't it? Deep-laid thought patterns tend to reproduce themselves in our imagination, sometimes waking us out of a deep sleep with a worried, uneasy feeling, seldom waking us with a song of joy. Yet always we are striving for this song, because something deep within us, deeper than all our experiences, seems to be telling us that everything is all right with the soul and that life would be good if we knew how to live it.

We used to think that we must be well in order to be happy. We now know, as one prominent physician has said, that we have to be happy if we wish to be well. In such degree as the mind is operating against itself, it makes the whole body unhappy. How can the feet dance unless the mind is nimble? How can the heart beat in rhythm with life when the mind is singing a hymn of hate or chanting a funeral dirge? How can the hands be steady and skillful if the mind is jumpy and timid? And how can people have hope unless they have faith?

Believe it or not, the Bible, particularly the New Testament, suggests a sure cure for the mental ills that give rise to so many of our physical troubles and certainly create all our unhappiness, our sense of insecurity, and our fear of life. In modern terms, we speak of the re-integration of the personality, and physicians trained in the field of psychiatry are spending their time taking people apart mentally and putting them together again.

What do we mean by the re-integration of a personality: by taking people apart mentally and putting them together again so they can function normally and happily? We mean that the thoughts and emotions that have been buried in the mind will be brought to the light of day and seen for exactly what they are—an accumulation of fears and doubts and uncertainties, an accumulation of a lack of faith and trust in oneself, in life, and in God, the power greater than we are.

In the science of psychiatry, all these deep-laid negative emotional experiences are brought to the surface so that patients may see themselves as they really are. The wonderful thing about this is that when a patient actually sees that they are suffering from pent up emotional repressions, the pressure of these buried thought images is released and the mind thinks again from the happy viewpoint of the child who hasn't learned to be afraid of life.

This doesn't mean that the patient is reduced to a point of infantile or childish reactions to life. It means rather that the original stream of the joy of living flows through them and into self-expression.

When this takes place, the patient is said to be re-integrated. Their personality has been taken apart and all the parts laid out before them and then reassembled in their proper place, so they function happily and harmoniously. The parts were already there, but like an automobile that has been taken down for repair and put together wrong, things don't synchronize. It puffs and starts and tries to go sideways and jumps up and down like a bucking bronco. Thought patterns do repeat themselves with monotonous regularity until they are changed.

I once knew a man who continuously heard a few bars of a certain piece of music day and night, until it nearly drove him crazy. He was an actor and traced the problem back to an experience he had in a studio where it was necessary that these certain bars be played over and over. At the time, he was discouraged, mentally low, and physically tired. He wasn't able to laugh off the experience. It got him down, so to speak, until finally the strains automatically repeated themselves.

He was rapidly going down the road of complete mental disintegration, and yet the remedy was simple enough. As soon as he saw what the trouble was, it was automatically corrected because he knew that his mind was not being interfered with by something other than itself. He came to see that he was in a self-imposed prison. A few simple affirmations a day repeated over a period of time completely healed him. The wonderful thing is that he really healed himself by getting back in rhythm with life.

When we speak of an integrated personality, we mean one that is adjusted to life and the way it has to live, one that flows along with the current of events. This doesn't mean one that is lazy in one's thought or indolent in one's acts. It merely means that one acts with harmony and happiness, one responds with joy and confidence.

But there is more to the re-integration of a personality than this. You and I wouldn't be here if we were not rooted in Spirit, because our mind is not separated from the mind of the universe; it is one with it. It is no idle statement to say that heaven is our home, because harmony is the great reality, love the great impulsion, and all our reactions must be based in harmony, in happiness, and in love if we are to get the most out of life.

We may seek to avoid this issue. We may try to laugh it off or completely deny its reality, but all to no avail. We do belong to the universe in which we live. We are some part of it. We do have a spiritual nature. Each one of us is Spirit, and the laws of our spiritual life work with the same accuracy that the laws of our mental and physical life do.

Jesus knew this better than we do, and he laid down the rules for the game of life as they ought to be played. He knew as well as we do that we have a physical body and that it must be properly cared for. He knew that we have an emotional reaction to life, because no one ever lived who had a deeper feeling than he had.

But Jesus knew something more that the world still has to discover. He knew that while we have a physical body that must be in right relationship to the mind, the mind also must be united with the

Spirit, from which can come only good, only peace, happiness, and love. Jesus made heaven and earth meet. He did not say heaven is reserved to you as a future good. He said, "Look around you, open your eyes, and you will see heaven, because it is here now." You and I know that this flatly contradicts much of our human experience, and yet as you look back over the pages of history, you do find that the people whose lives we try to pattern after, the ones whom the world takes as models for right thought and conduct, were the ones Jesus was talking about in that most eloquent sermon ever delivered, the Sermon on the Mount.

Are we empty of every good thing? Does mind and heart cry out ceaselessly, day and night, because of peace? Jesus said, "Blessed are they who do hunger and thirst after righteousness, because they will be filled." He didn't say that *maybe* they will be filled, or they *ought* to be filled, or perhaps *someday* they will become filled. He said, "Blessed is their fulfillment *today*." He said, "The meek will inherit the earth" and "the peacemakers will be called the children of God." We have avoided the issue too long. It is never too late, although it is later than we think.

There is no complete reintegration of the personality without some form of spiritual life. You may call it a creed, a doctrine, a religion, or any other name you see fit, but neither science nor philosophy nor all human knowledge can alter the fact that we are rooted in pure Spirit. This is why it is that today as never before in all history, a great cry goes up from the heart of humanity, a cry of fear mingled with despair, because the world is in a state of confusion. It has lost its spiritual moorings. Its boat is rocked on the waves of uncertainty. Its hope flounders on the rocks of insecurity until faith itself seems submerged in a sea of confusion.

It is amazing that we have radio and television and wireless, that we have nylon stockings and refrigerators, that we can fly across the ocean in a few hours and destroy the largest city with a few bombs. How marvelous is humankind's ingenuity, and how terrific the impact of scientific discovery on the life of the whole world!

Why, then, the fear? Unless it is that knowledge without wisdom is like action without hope, containing within itself the seed of futility. It is not that we should desire less knowledge. It is wonderful to think that I can be sitting here in this studio and speaking to you. It is wonderful to me that you are kind enough to listen. But to what end is modern invention, to what purpose is this vast knowledge, without wisdom? Wisdom alone causes people to use knowledge for good purposes.

It seems as though the whole human mind were at mischief today, and it is my sincere conviction, without the slightest fear, that the time has come when wisdom must stand at the helm, that our knowledge will not find its boat wrecked for lack of a true compass and guide.

I have seen too many lives happily re-integrated by coming sincerely, simply, and directly to believe that God is still in God's heaven. I have seen too many people resurrected from fear and uncertainty by coming to know that there is a power greater than they are, upon which they may rely, to doubt what could happen to the world if a sufficient number of people should unite their faith in one common accord.

God is still the answer to human need. God is still the common denominator of human desire, and some form of spiritual enlightenment and understanding is still the only cure for the whole world. It is your privilege, and mine, to learn to practice the presence of God in everything we do, trusting that we will be led by divine guidance. Having faith in the power of good, let us "advance, and advance on chaos and the night."

THE NEXT VOICE YOU HEAR

The next voice you hear might be God's. Wouldn't it be wonderful if this were true? Wouldn't it be wonderful if we could hear the voice of God? Perhaps we can. Perhaps we all have heard the voice of God but haven't recognized it.

Recently, I was invited to the preview of a motion picture called *The Next Voice You Hear*, produced by Dore Schary at Metro-Gold-wyn-Mayer studios. I was so impressed by the production and the wonderful way in which Mr. Schary had worked it out that I asked his consent to use the idea of his story.

In this motion picture, God is supposed to go on an international radio circuit to warn the world that it must change its way of thinking and living if it is to survive and if humankind is to achieve those miracles of love and faith necessary to the well being of all humanity—the miracle of peace, of happiness and compassion, of cooperation and of mutual benefit.

In the picture, God's voice, which of course is never heard directly as an audible voice, is personally heard by everyone who listens in. Everyone hears the voice in their own language, even though all nationalities are listening to the same broadcast.

Mr. Schary chose as the characters for this production a typical American family, a family with its petty differences of opinion, its little controversies, and its great love for each other. Just the average family, wondering, as we all do: What is it all about? Is life a comedy or a tragedy? Does it have a meaning? Is there a common denominator for faith? Why is it that we are afraid of God? Do we believe in God?

I asked Mr. Schary how he happened to make this picture. He was intrigued with the idea in the original material that everyone could hear the same voice, but each in a different language. He was fascinated by the thought that if we all could actually hear this inward voice, it would change the current of human events.

It is, as Mr. Schary said, the nature of humankind to seek God, and so, throughout the ages, religions have been formed that fit the needs of some particular way of belief. But whatever the form any religion takes, the purpose is always the same. Always it is based on an inward conviction common to all people that there is a supreme intelligence guiding the universe and that there is a real need for communion between God and the individual.

The ways in which we approach God are as different as our own individualities, but the purpose is always identical: to reach out toward a power greater than we are; and to seek the guidance of an intelligence that can direct our paths into ways of prosperity and peace. There is only one God, and this God is, or should become, an immediate experience in our lives. We all should hear the voice of God, not a God who was, but the God who is.

The Next Voice You Hear tells what happened when one night the voice of God was heard on the radio. It was heard in all lands and in all languages and at the same time, and it is the purpose of this picture to show what happens to people of every country and every culture who actually hear this inward voice which comes to all in their own tongue, because God is the God of all. God is in the hearts of all people.

Mr. Schary felt that the story of *The Next Voice You Hear* should be told not only about God, but about the individual, who is the spiritual image and likeness of God. The individual is of like nature with God, and so the story is told about a person listening to God—the average person in an average house in an average community—and here the picture departs from the ordinary procedure and does away with all spectacles and camera tricks, which, as Mr. Schary told me, might dazzle but do not really persuade.

It should be a source of great satisfaction to know that where this picture has been shown, it has produced an astounding effect. And no wonder, since it assumes what all people long for—a direct relationship to God. It assumes that we do inwardly hear the voice of God, and we hear it in our own mind, as though some divine intuition had forevermore implanted spiritual truth at the very center of our own being.

So this picture takes as its central figure just the average American citizen, just an ordinary citizen of the world anywhere, trying to find out what it is all about, what the meaning of life is.

But it instructs as well as entertains, since it clearly shows that the popular concept of the fear of God merely means that we are intimidated and over-awed, and our fear of God has stood in the way of getting closer to God in faith. The whole motive of the picture is to show that love is stronger than fear, that fear tends to alienate us one from another, while love and understanding bring us closer together. God is not a God of wrath, of fire and brimstone, but a God of love, a God intimately associated with everything that lives, and we need not fear God.

We all have our fears, our doubts, and our anxieties, and above and behind these, we all have something else, something that we didn't put there—an inward voice, the voice of God within us. We are all searching after this something, not knowing that it is within all people, this something that can make us whole as individuals and bring us all together in a community of Spirit.

If we are to do this, we must find some common denominator, some universal acceptance on which all may agree. This common denominator will have to speak a common language. It will have to speak to us directly in our own thought, from our own hearts. Our little and petty differences of opinion will have to be washed out in the cleansing flood of some divine wave that emerges from the ocean of life.

We all have much more in common than we have realized. Every normal person in the world loves someone. Love, then, is a common denominator. It speaks a thousand different tongues, but it always emanates from the same source. How could there be such a common experience throughout the ages unless God were love—"a love so limitless, deep, and broad that we have renamed it and called it *God*"?

Since we want to get right down to the simple, everyday things of life, there is a common denominator even in a smile. If you were to go into the deepest jungle or walk down the sidewalks of a great city, if you were to visit people of different cultures using different languages, and if you were to smile at them, they will smile back at you. A smile is a common denominator. A friendly handclasp is a common denominator. An act of kindness is a common denominator. Human goodness is a common denominator.

In *The Next Voice You Hear*, you find a person at the head of a family that he loves, but who is so filled with antagonism and resistance that he has become impatient with everything around him. He thinks his boss is against him. He dislikes his relatives. He is irritated with the traffic cop, and because of this, he is fighting his world. It is only when the voice of God comes to him in the only way it can come to any of us—as that inner, silent feeling that all this changed—that he is able to see behind all differences to that one constant reality, the common denominator, the presence of good everywhere.

As he experiences the change that takes place in his own life through hearing the voice and recognizing it, he finds that others have had the same experience. They, too, have been listening, and as he learns to meet them on this new basis of understanding, he finds that they become friendly and cooperative.

The Next Voice You Hear is the story of all of us—of you and me and everyone else. It is the story of our lives as we actually live them. It is the story of our silent hopes and ambitions, our frustrations and failures, our wants and needs. There is something prophetic, almost awe-inspiring, about it.

Suppose, in our imagination, we should conceive of the voice of God coming over every radio in the world at an identical time for a whole week, and suppose this voice were actually to say, "You are following the wrong path. You are following the path that leads to ruin. But there is still time. The hour is late, but not too late."

I suppose this is the most dramatic thought that could come to us, that countless millions of human beings around the world should hear the same voice at the same time. And yet no physical voice is ever recorded. It is an inward voice that is heard—a deep feeling that wells up from the heart of humanity, a great yearning toward something that can bind up the wounds of the world and make it whole again.

What do you think would happen if this could actually take place? What would happen in your own life, what would you do about it, what would I do about it, if we really heard this voice? I think at least we should stop and look and listen and begin to wonder, and somehow or other I feel that it would change our manner of living. We would come to see that the things of real value in life are the common experiences we share with each other—the hope, the love, the trust, and the friend-ship that we all have need of.

Of course, the movie *The Next Voice You Hear* is a fantasy. It is entertainment. It is just another show. But wait a moment—is it? It was more than this to me, and I know it was infinitely more than this to those who sat near me, and why did it make such an impression on all of us unless it had touched some deep well-spring of life within us waiting to be tapped?

We all not only wish to hear the voice of God, we all actually believe that there is such a voice—or to put it in a more abstract form, such a presence—and this voice, or this presence, is personal to each of us. It comes to each in a little different way, but, coming from the same source, it tells us all the same thing. It tells us that God had made all people out of the same material, putting within each one of us a spark of God's own life. It tells us that there is only one race, which is the human race, that faith is the common denominator of all religions, and that each one of us must set up what Emerson called a "lowly listening" to the great heart of reality, and it tells us what will happen when we do this.

It is because *The Next Voice You Hear* is created out of deep spiritual conviction that it arouses the same conviction within us. Personally, I do not believe that such things happen merely by chance, because whenever there is a great need in the world, God stands ready to an-swer that need, and there surely is a need in the world today that we will all better understand each other, that we will learn of the tolerance and the love that are necessary to get along together, and that we will all join in one common faith.

God has already done God's part. God has given us a life to live. God has given us the imagination to feel it and the will to live it and the intellect to understand at least some part of it, and God has implanted within everyone a sort of divine memory of who and what

169

God is and where God came from—"that celestial palace whence God came."

We are all very much like the prodigal of old who finally remembered that in his father's house was peace, happiness, and abundance, and so the young man resolutely set his face toward home, and on the return journey, the miracle of life and love took place. The father saw him afar off and came out to meet him. There was no harsh judgment, no condemnation, no asking where he had been or what he had been doing or why he had been away. Instead, he felt the soft embrace of loving arms, the glad welcome of a loving heart, and found reunion with the family that is both the family of God and the family of humankind—just the ordinary family, just the average citizen, just you and me and God.

What Do You
See in the Mirror?

Sometime ago I read a short article called "The Scent of Fear," in which it was claimed that fear exudes a scent that an animal can smell. The author claimed that this scent of fear arouses an antagonism within the animal, and it often attacks in self-defense.

I once knew a geologist who told me that he was sitting on a rock one day out in the desert, drawing a map. As he worked, he happened to glance down and notice a rattlesnake coiled under the edge of the rock on which he was sitting. I asked him what he did when he saw the rattlesnake, and if was he afraid of it. He said, "Not at all. I had no desire to hurt the snake, and it had no desire to harm me." So he sat there and leisurely completed his plans and then went about his business with no thought of fear.

This reminded me of a passage in the Bible that says, "Behold, I give unto you power to tread on serpents and scorpions, and over all the power of the enemy; and nothing will by any means hurt you." And in another place, "They will take up serpents; and if they drink any deadly thing, it will not hurt them; they will lay hands on the sick, and they will recover."

I'm not sure that I would be willing to pick up a rattlesnake, but I do know that I love dogs, and I have never had a dog so much as snap at me. They certainly do feel your personal atmosphere, and if it is one of trust and confidence, if it is one of understanding and love, they will respond to it.

We are not dogs and we are not rattlesnakes, but I wonder if it is true—and I feel certain that it is—that when we have an atmosphere of antagonism toward others, they inwardly feel it and their response to us will be antagonistic. Perhaps this is why the Bible says that a soft answer turns away wrath.

We are all human beings trying to get along with each other, trying to find out how to live happily together, trying to cooperate in the great game of life, and we don't always succeed as well as we would like to. There is a subtle atmosphere around each one of us that, without our knowing it, is silently attracting people to us or repelling them from us, and I have no doubt that some form of fear is the cause of most of our troubles. What the animal smells because of its acute instinct, we humans feel inwardly when we contact each other.

Moreover, I believe that an atmosphere of failure actually attracts failure, and I know that those who always have the feeling that no one likes them surround themselves with an atmosphere that pushes people away from them, but they don't know just how or why. Just as an animal smells fear, people sense the feeling of those around them. It seems as though our mental attitudes are contagious, as though we go around more or less enveloped in them, and the silent influence we exercise on others is something that takes place automatically. Friendship attracts friends, while antagonism not only repels people but actually awakens a feeling of distrust and dislike within them.

Here is one of the keys to successful living and right relationships among people. It is only when we are whole within ourselves that we can help others. It is only when we have faith that we can instill faith. It is only when we have hope and enthusiasm that others respond to us with an equal hope and enthusiasm.

You have often noticed that when you spend considerable time with people who are depressed and afraid, you feel as though the weight of the universe was on your shoulders, as though everything was hopeless. On the other hand, in company with those who are buoyant and confident, you feel a lightness, a sense of joy, a feeling of enthusiasm.

It is almost as definite as going from fog to sunshine and from sunshine back into fog again. It is as definite as the wind in your face. Sometimes, as you have talked with people who are depressed and tried to bring them comfort and courage, you have felt their atmosphere lift, just as though the fog were clearing away. You feel the sun coming out again, and almost invariably these people will tell you how much better they feel for having talked with you.

We all would like to establish a sense of confidence, an atmosphere of faith, and a feeling of good fellowship that will keep us happy and make others happy, and I believe it will also attract us to those situations that make for a successful life. If we can get it into our minds that people and conditions around us, as far as we are concerned, are largely reflections of our own mental attitudes, we will arrive at the right place to begin a more constructive program for living.

If we could really come to see that life is like a mirror, always tending to reflect back to us the images of our own thinking, then we should realize that by changing our thinking, we can change the reflections in the mirror. The next question would be: What do we want to see in this mirror? And have we the courage to admit that what we are looking at in the mirror is a reflected image of our own outlook on life? Are we looking at antagonism, resentment, or confusion? Are we looking at fear, failure, or unhappiness? Are we actually willing to look into this mirror of life and say, "That is me."? And if we don't like what we see, have we enough confidence to believe that we can change it? If so, we have made the right start.

It isn't going to do any good to condemn ourselves because of what we see in the mirror, because that would only make matters worse. What we have to do is to get a vision of something better. It is just as wrong to condemn ourselves as it is for us to condemn others. For instance, when Jesus said you should love your neighbor as yourself, he did not imply that you should hate yourself in order to love others. Quite the opposite. He said to think as well of others as you do of yourself.

No doubt Jesus knew that, way down in our minds, we are really thinking of others as we think of ourselves, with the same hope or the same disappointment, the same love or the same dislike. Really, Jesus implied that you should think well of yourself, and he was referring to that deep self within each of us that is already one with God.

We should come to love the God within us and see the same God within others. Then we should actually be loving our neighbor as ourselves, because we are both included in the great scheme of things. Our starting point is to recognize God at the center of our own being, to have faith in this divine presence within us, and to have an equal faith in the divine in everyone else. We must come to see that God is the one eternal presence in everyone and in everything, and we must learn to think from this basis.

How wonderful it would be if we were never afraid of anything. We are afraid of people because we think in some way they can harm us. So the very antagonism we have for others arouses a like antagonism from them to us. But turn the proposition around, change fear into faith and antagonism into love, and we will have reversed the whole process.

The mirror is merely something that reflects. You couldn't scratch the reflection out of the mirror. You can only change the image in front of it, and you are the image maker. So forget the mirror, and create new images that will reflect new patterns, and make this very definite. Bring it down to earth, because theories are no good unless they are applied.

Let us take the example of those people who feel that everyone is against them. They always seem to be at cross purposes with people and with events. This has gone on until other people actually avoid them because they feel the resentment in their minds, and it arouses an equal antagonism in other people's thoughts about them.

Let's make believe that we are teaching these people what is actually taking place, and let's make believe that they are accepting our explanation. Here is the key to this situation. You and I understand what is wrong with people who feel that everyone is against them. We know that their suffering is self-imposed, and we wish to help them. So our explanation will have to be very kind and considerate. It will have to be like leading a child or helping an invalid, because they really are sick people. We are going to act as a doctor to their mind, and doctors do not harshly judge their patients. They try to help and encourage them to the place where the great restoring power of nature can resume its natural function.

You and I are acting as a physician to these people's minds. We, too, will have to be kind and considerate and willing to let them explode a little, be willing even for them to be antagonistic to our approach, because we understand what is eating at the vitals of their being. Way down there, they are afraid, scared to death, and unconsciously they are reacting in self-defense. This we must explain to them.

I want to tell you that in many year's experience, I have never yet met a single person who won't "take it" if you approach them in the right spirit, because way down inside, everyone is longing for love and friendship. We would rather have love and friendship than anything else in the world. We want people to like us. Some people are afraid of people, that is all! So let's tell these people how the mind works and how it is that they must come to have faith in something bigger than they are. This they will like, because they are looking for strength. They long for happiness, as blind people long for light.

We are going to be very gentle about this, with the simple, sincere desire to be helpful and with no criticism whatsoever. We might even say—and no doubt it would have considerable truth in it—that there was a time when we felt exactly as they do. We thought everything was against us. But one day the light broke, and gradually a transformation took place in our lives, and now we feel that we share our secret with them, and we can take them by the hand and they will respond with confidence.

The change may not take place in a day, a week, or a month, but it will take place if we persist. Let us give these people certain affirmations to make every day, and let us help them to make these affirmations. Let us make them with them. Then they will feel that they have a partner, and this is a feeling we all need. They have someone who understands them. It won't be long before they will be working with us with an enthusiasm equal to our own, and, by and by, the signs will begin to follow. Their mirror will begin to change its reflection.

This will create hope, and it is only a short step from hope to faith. Through this experience, we will learn the great lesson of life, that the good we have must be shared with others if it is to be increased. When you have made a friend with someone who is friendless and made it possible for them to acquire friends, you have multiplied your own friendship by that number of people. When you have brought good to someone else and shown them how to extend that good in their own experience, you have brought that much more good into your own life.

LET'S TRY FAITH

The Bible tells us that "faith is the substance of things hoped for, the evidence of things not seen." Throughout the ages, there have been people whose faith has proved that there is a spiritual power that we can use. It was his complete belief in this power, his absolute reliance on it, and his conscious use of it for every purpose, that made Jesus the outstanding spiritual teacher of all the ages. When we read the words of Jesus, we realize that he had complete reliance on this spiritual power and that he based everything he did on his understanding of it, his acceptance of it, and his use of it.

For instance, he would say to one who was sick, "Do you believe that I can heal you?" And then, when the person said, "Yes," Jesus would say, "Your faith has made you whole." He told his followers that if they had faith the size of a grain of mustard seed, which is one of the smallest of all seeds, they could remove mountains of obstruction.

When the Bible said that faith is the substance of things hoped for and the evidence of things not seen, it was plainly stating that our faith does actually lay hold of a spiritual power that is real substance. It is

177

not an illusory or a visionary "something," but an actual substance in the universe, a paver that really exists and that we can consciously use.

Faith is such a substance, and the Bible tells us that when we have faith, we will see the evidence that this substance actually exists. That is, our faith will produce a real, tangible result. Here, the word *evidence* is used in a literal, practical sense, and the statement means exactly what it says when it tells us, as Jesus did, that definite physical signs will follow our belief. "These signs will follow them that believe." Again, Jesus said that whatsoever things you ask for when you pray, if you believe that you have them, you will receive them.

There has been plenty of proof of this power of faith throughout the ages, and we are receiving plenty of proof of it through people's responses to this philosophy. I have thousands of letters that testify to the power of faith. Personally, if I had never known of the power of faith before, I would be completely convinced by the mail I have received during the last twelve or fifteen months. It is impossible to escape this conviction, because there is actual proof of thousands of cases where people have prayed believing, or prayed affirmatively, which means they have accepted the answer to their own spiritual affirmations, they have come to believe that they are dealing with an actual law of good that acts in their behalf, and they have received the proof of it. The old saying that the proof of the pudding is in the eating is just as true in this as in other things.

So it seems to me that in our desire and attempt to help ourselves and each other, and help the whole world, there could be nothing more important for us to do than to develop a great affirmative faith, a faith in something greater than we are, in a law of good that responds to us so completely that we can actually touch and handle the results, whether it is in better health or more prosperous circumstances or happier conditions in living.

Our faith in spiritual things is not to be used only on rare occasions, when the need is so great. We ought to use our faith every day, in everything we do. We are so likely to think that some things are little and others are big that we sometimes forget that to God all things are possible and that God knows nothing about hard and easy or big and little. The power that you and I are using in our prayer of affirmation is an absolute power. It is complete, perfect, and self-acting.

But again, let us ask, "Just what is faith?" Let's analyze its meaning and reduce it to something so basic that we can understand it, and let's keep it simple.

Let's begin by realizing that faith is a certain way of thinking. Faith is an affirmation of our belief. If it is to have power, it must be even more than an affirmation; it must be the recognition of a power that actually exists and an inward realization that this power is set in motion through our belief in it.

Next, we should realize that faith acts as a positive law in the universe, something that asserts itself just as all other laws do. The funny thing about this is, we already have this kind of faith in pretty nearly everything in life, but when it comes to having faith in spiritual things or faith in God, we become confused in our minds because we think that faith is so intangible. It seems like such an elusive thing, so invisible and so intangible. This is why the Bible statement says that faith is substance, it is evidence, it is reality, it is law and order, it is a truth that demonstrates itself and provides us with an evidence of its reality.

It is this evidence that we all need and should have. You and I have a right to know that our prayers of faith will be answered. We have a right to know that positive faith produces definite and positive results, and we must come to believe that we can use this faith in the simplest things in life, that we can use it for ourselves and others and for the whole world. We must think the thing through until we have this conviction in our minds, and then we must use it until we experience the evidence of its reality. Our motto should be: "To know is to do, and to do is to know."

If you were praying for someone who needed physical healing, and if, in your meditation for them, you are affirming that there is a perfect Spirit within them and that this Spirit is flowing through their physical being and restoring it to health, there should be a betterment in their physical condition, and there will be. That betterment will be equal to your faith in the presence of God within them, your affirmation of the reality of that presence, and your own inward realization of the meaning of the words you use.

If you are praying for a betterment in someone's circumstances, following the teaching of the one who really knew when he said that when you pray, believe that you have and you will receive, then you must believe that the words you use in your affirmation are acted on by a power greater than you are, a power that can and will produce actual results in this person's circumstances. For instance, if you are praying for someone to be more prosperous, and your prayer is effective, that person will become more prosperous. New things will begin to happen to them and new opportunities will be presented to them.

We already use such a natural law when we plant an acorn and expect an oak, or plant a kernel of corn and expect an ear of corn, because we know that there is a creative substance that converts the seed into the plant and causes the plant to bear fruit. The interesting thing about this is that we do not help the process very much. We merely provide the proper conditions through which the law may operate.

Now suppose we exercise the same faith in our meditations and in our affirmative prayers, and let's say that the meditation or the prayer is like the seed falling into the substance of the soil that is going to give us evidence through the plant. All we have to do is to exercise this same faith. As the Bible says, "Through faith, we understand that the world is framed by the word of God, so that things which are seen were not made of things which do appear."

*This is a wonderful statement. Through faith, the things that we see come out of an invisible substance that we do not see, and the substance provides an evidence that we do see.

The Bible clearly states that the whole physical universe is a result of the word of God, or the thought of God. Moses said that the creative word is in our own mouth, that we should know it and do it, and Jesus said that if you believe, it will be done unto you. Here are two of the most challenging statements in the Bible.

In a certain sense, they are the two most inspiring thoughts in all the literature of all the ages. If the Bible had never given us any other two thoughts than these, it would still have been the greatest book in existence.

Somehow or other we have overlooked, or not quite comprehended, their meaning. We haven't taken them literally enough. They have been used as sort of symbols of hope rather than the actual realization of a spiritual presence and a spiritual law so close to us that it flows through our thinking and so present everywhere that it creates and governs all things.

Can anything be more wonderful that this, that you and I, unknown, unhonored, and unsung, do still carry with us, in what the Bible calls the secret place of the Most High, the solution to every problem, the answer to every need, the possibility of using a power that can do anything? But as wonderful as this is, it isn't enough. Perhaps we are like people who have a large sum of money deposited in the bank but don't realize they can draw a check on it. God has already deposited this power within us; we had nothing to do with it whatsoever. But God cannot use it for us. This we will have to do for ourselves.

It is so important that we do this, because if there is anything the world needs today it is proof of spiritual power, both individually and collectively. If all of us who accept the possibility of faith were to use such conviction as we have, unitedly, a spiritual inspiration would come to the world that, as it worked out through people and events, would readjust all differences. A law of good that will work in and through the life of an individual will work with the same power in and through a group of individuals, and the world is a group of individuals.

There is enough spiritual conviction in the world today, if it were properly used, to settle all national and international disputes, to produce a just and lasting peace, and to bring prosperity and happiness to the whole world. This power will have to be used if this tremendous good is to be brought about. Since there is only one place where you and I can begin, which is in our own minds, should we not all take definite time each day to call on this power of good, to feel its presence and actually to use it for the whole world?

It is an interesting thing that our leaders everywhere are asking us to do this. Whether it is the head of the Catholic Church or the Protestant Church or the Synagogue, or the spiritual leaders in India, or whether it is our military and political leaders and educators, they are all beseeching us to use such spiritual power as we have for the benefit of the world.

This is the most promising sign of the times, that the world, in the midst of such terrific confusion and uncertainty, should have reached a place where leaders everywhere unitedly ask for the prayers of those who do believe. Somehow or other they are reaching out instinctively to a power greater than they are.

So let's learn to have faith, and, having it, let's learn to use it. And using it, let's expect results. If we were depending only on our individual will or our little self-determination or our little ego, we couldn't expect very much. But this is exactly what we are *not* depending on. We are depending on a power greater than we are, a presence that fills all space, that creates everything, and that is at the center of our own being. We are calling on the power of God in human affairs. We are asking the divine maker of all things to remold our lives.

Peace can come out of this confusion, and joy can come out of this sorrow, and if we only give our consent, the divine Spirit can and will govern human affairs.

SPIRITUAL SELF-RELIANCE

One of our great needs is that we believe in ourselves, in what we are doing, and in our own destiny. No one could have convinced either Jesus or Gandhi that they were unable to accomplish what they set out to do. Self-reliance finds its greatest outlet when it is accompanied by a high vision as well as a quiet determination.

Let us see if we cannot analyze what self-reliant people do, how they think, and what is behind their convictions.

First of all, the person with spiritual self-reliance must believe in God. History shows that it makes no great difference what people with spiritual self-reliance may have believed as far as their different types of religious faiths were concerned, because fundamental to all faith is the belief in God. Everything else is non-essential. It is the belief in God that gives the background. All people with spiritual self-reliance have had a deep and an abiding conviction that they were one with the divine Spirit.

This is right where you and I will have to begin if we wish to develop spiritual self-reliance, something that will make us positive without aggressiveness, something that will make us completely sure of ourselves without egotism, and something that will make us positive in action without becoming intolerant. This something is a complete and abiding faith in the two principle factors that make for spiritual self-reliance and creative living.

First of all, and fundamental to everything else, is the faith in God, and next, and equally necessary, is faith in ourselves. The kind of faith in ourselves we are talking about is, of course, not in an isolated self, as though we were struggling alone, but rather faith in a spiritual self, because this type of self-reliance comes only to those who have a deep conviction not only about God, but about themselves. Therefore, this kind of self-reliance must have as one of the mainsprings for its being the conviction that we, as a living spirit, move and have our being in God.

The kind of spiritual self-reliance we are talking about is a reliance on ourselves because we first know that the real self is, as the Bible so beautifully states, "hid with Christ in God," which means that every person's nature is divine. We are rooted in the Infinite. We live because God lives in us. We think because the mind of God thinks through us, and we are able to act creatively because the mind that created everything is creating something new in us.

All false egotism goes when a true understanding of the real ego dawns on us. If we know that we are one with something bigger than we are, then we will realize that everything necessary to our life is already within us. And so we find that the great spiritual geniuses of the ages have spent much time alone with themselves and with God. Whether you choose to call this fasting and prayer or meditation makes no difference.

Here are the first steps, then, in acquiring spiritual self-reliance: to believe in God with the intensity of your whole being; to believe in the reality of your spiritual self as forever one with God; and to establish a continual communion with the God, who is both within and around you.

Last, but not least, we find that all these great souls acted on their vision. Having received it, they no longer remained passive. They carried the vision into action in human affairs. They were like perennial mountain tops that flowed down into the valleys to irrigate the land. They were like people who listen to some celestial song in the silence of their own souls and then sing it over again that others might hear. They were like those who went into the secret place of the Most High within themselves and received the healing balm of life, then took it into the marketplace so that others could be made whole.

Jesus applied his spiritual power for every sort of definite and specific purpose. The healing of the sick, the feeding the multitude, and all the other miraculous things that took place in his experience were a direct result of having followed the first three rules fundamental to acquiring spiritual self-reliance: Believe in God; Believe in your spiritual self; Commune with God. Talk to God, let God talk to you, and then, out of the inspiration that comes, carry this power and this conviction into the affairs of everyday living.

Let us see how this would work out in our own experience, and let's start with the suppositional case of those who lack confidence in themselves, those who have no self-reliance whatsoever. These people think of themselves as weak and inadequate, filled with fear and disappointment. They are frustrated because their fondest hopes have been shattered on the rocks of experience. Their boat is adrift on an ocean of uncertainty. It seems as though there were no chart, no compass, no guide, no pilot, only aimless and uncertain drifting.

We have described a pretty forlorn hope, haven't we? At least the prodigal child of the Bible is as far away from home as he can ever get, and it was right there, in that distant land, in that faraway place, that something within which he hadn't put there, something that God had put there, caused him to remember who and what he was. It doesn't matter what his experience may have been or where he may now be, he has this divine memory. God made him. God is everywhere and has never wandered away from him. The Divine is forever speaking, but perhaps the prodigal hasn't been listening.

Something within the prodigal remembers and seems to whisper to him that things might be different. This is hope, coming like a gleam of light from an invisible lighthouse, and the prodigal will do well to listen. It is very apparent in the story that the prodigal did listen. He communed with God because everything else had failed. He listened to God because everything else he had been hearing was false and confusing.

Just what had happened to him at this point? Up until now, he had been out on his own, alone. He had become frustrated and destitute, and then, at long last, he had begun to think, to listen, to talk to the something that he dimly remembered, just as we all do. And that "something" responded to him and brought with it a vision, the vision of a better life, the vision of a parental house, of loving associates and a home for which he so greatly longed.

Suppose that everything had stopped right here. He would have merely had a beautiful dream, a dream from which he must so soon awake only to find himself plunged more deeply into despair. He had followed the first three conclusions we have described: he had come to believe in God (possibly he had never stopped believing in God, but he had come to have a new faith and confidence and something that hadn't happened to him before); he discovered that he had a spiritual self, that he himself was one with God, and had listened; and, listening, he had received certain instructions.

Now a new determination came to him—the will to act, backed by the impulse of his faith. A whole new energy flowed into him, a feeling and an imagination.

But even this wasn't enough, because the will to act must be followed by the action, so that the will itself passes into its own action and becomes the act. It is only in this way that we hook up desire, feeling, and creativity with accomplishment. So the prodigal arose and started on the return journey.

Like ourselves, certain doubts assailed him. Would his father receive him? Had he strength enough to make the journey? Since there were thieves on the highway, what enemies would he encounter on the road? What deserts must he pass through in the heat of the day? What mountains must he climb? What rivers must be forded? It seems as though every obstruction the imagination could conceive confronted him. But the vision did not die. The confidence in the newly discovered faith was fresh and strong and clear. Even the most deadly attitude of all, which is self-condemnation, finally fled when his father enfolded him in a loving embrace.

You can see that this is the story of all of us—you and me and everyone. It is the story of human life, the greatest story ever told, but any without meaning whatsoever until we personalize it. We are that prodigal, and so our experiment is with ourselves, as it always must be. What difference does it make if we have floundered and failed? Now that we remember, let us arise. Let us awaken this sleeping giant within us, this spiritual genius who is forevermore one with God.

Let's trust this divine partnership as we have never trusted anything else. For everything that says, "No," let's find a "Yes." When the thought comes that says, "I cannot," let's say, "But God can." That within me, which is pure Spirit, can and will. If the thought comes that says, "Behold all these obstructions," let's say, "God knows no obstruction." The Spirit within you—your real self—knows no obstruction, and for every mental argument that denies you the good that you feel belongs to your real self, see to it that you find an affirmation that counteracts it.

You need not be afraid, because a faith is forming itself in you, a faith that can overcome anything, a conviction that no longer doubts, a feeling that reaches out into the invisible and grasps power in its hands, draws it into your experience, and expresses it in your act, and gradually a conviction will come to you that will turn all obstructions into opportunities, all fear into faith, and all doubt into certainty.

Humankind's
Greatest Discovery

The greatest discovery ever made about humankind is the discovery of the creative power of thought, how your thought can help in healing your body and how it can help you to control the circumstances and situations around you. Thousands of books have been written on this subject, and there are probably ten or fifteen million people in this country who are trying to use the creative power of their thought for definite purposes.

With due modesty, I might even say that several of my own books have for years been among the best sellers in this field, and they have all dealt with the creative power of thinking. Millions of magazines are printed each month for those who believe in the creative power of thought and who are trying to use it. There would not be such a vast inquiry and eager attention unless there were a great truth involved.

The relationship of our thinking to what happens to us, both in our bodily health and our circumstances, is one of the greatest discoveries we have ever made. But if we were to ask, "How is thought creative?" we couldn't answer the question any more than, "Why does a chicken come out of an egg?" or "Why do acorns become oak trees?" or "Why does gravity hold everything in place?" When we discover a principle in nature, we have to accept it. We cannot explain why thought is creative, but we can accept the fact and see what we can do with it.

We are operated on by mental and spiritual forces, just as we are operated on by physical ones. Just as gravitational force holds a physical object in the place we set it, so there is another kind of force that operates on our thinking and tends to bring into our experience those things that we hold in mind.

This will explain why faith is effective, because faith is a positive mental and emotional acceptance, an affirmative attitude of mind that uses the great creative power of thought constructively. It will also show why some prayers are answered and others are not. It gives us a key—and I believe a right one—to the teachings of Jesus about prayer.

Jesus said that when we pray, we should believe that we already have what we pray for. He said when you pray, believe that you receive, and you will have. When he said, "It is not I, but the Creator that dwells in me; the Creator does the works," was he not implying that there is in everyone a divine creative principle that everyone can make conscious use of?

We might say, if we move our furniture around in the room, "It is not I, but gravity that holds the different pieces of furniture in place." The only part we play is in shifting the furniture and setting it in the position we wish it to remain in. This is our individual freedom. We can use the laws of nature consciously and decide what we want them to do for us, but we are not these laws. They are greater than we are, and we may have implicit confidence in them because we know they will never let us down.

We know that when we plant a certain kind of seed, we will get a certain kind of plant. We know that when we mix certain colors together, we will get another color. We do the planting and the mixing, but nature produces the results. If we can keep these simple thoughts in mind and come to realize that the creative power of our thought is a power that we take out of nature rather than put in, it will be a great help to us. This is exactly as it should be, because you and I, with our little wills and our small imaginations and our personal opinions, have neither the intelligence nor the knowledge to always know what is best.

Jesus knew that no one can set themselves up in opposition to the laws of God and hope to succeed. But Jesus also knew something else. He knew that the laws of God are to be used. He knew that they ought to be used, and he knew that freedom comes when we use them rightly. To Jesus, spiritual laws were just as real as physical ones are to us. He knew that there is a silent, invisible, creative force that acts on us and through us at all times, whether we believe it or not, and his purpose and mission in life was to show us, first, that these laws exist; next, what they are and how they work; and thirdly, how to use them in such a way that only good will result.

Jesus never said that it is wrong to be happy. He never intimated that God wishes us to be sick or poor or disconsolate. Quite the reverse. Jesus used spiritual power for every conceivable purpose, for what we call small things as well as for what we call big things. He said that everything he did was an example for us to follow and that if we followed his example, definite signs would follow our belief, our faith, and our acceptance.

In coming to use these laws, then, for definite purposes, we should start with this fundamental proposition in mind: There is a law of good that operates on our thinking. There is a power greater than I am working for me. This power is good. This power is right where I am, operating in my thought now. I am not responsible for the power. I do not have to make it work. I do not have to beg it or intrigue it or coerce it. I merely use it.

If, then, we can come to see that such a law exists and that we are using a power greater than we are, we will at once be relieved of any sense of responsibility about it, as though we had to make it work. We do not sit around holding thoughts or trying to compel things to happen. As a matter of fact, this would defeat the very purpose we wish to accomplish. We no more make this law creative than we compel an acorn to become an oak. We do not hold thoughts over the acorn, nor do we visualize an oak tree. What we do is to plant an acorn and let nature create the oak tree for us.

This invisible force was real to Jesus. He had implicit faith in it. And because he did, all those things that have seemed so miraculous to the ages followed. He was a spiritual scientist who had come to understand that there is a universal principle of mind, a creative intelligence that acted on his faith and conviction, and that acted on this faith and conviction for definite purposes. He could tell the paralyzed to get up and walk, turn the water into wine, multiply the loaves and fishes by a process that, to him, was just as natural as it would be for us to use any of the laws of nature with which we are familiar.

It was his faith in these laws that gave him the power he had, because Jesus did not possess a power that other people do not have. He used a power that all people have but which few people make use of. He plainly told those around him that they could do the same thing. Some of his immediate followers experienced the same miraculous signs following their belief, and throughout the ages these signs have followed many people's belief.

To understand that faith is operated on by a natural law gives us the key to the whole situation. But it isn't enough to believe in a principle. This is only the starting point. Principles have to be used if they are going to produce definite results for us, and whether the principles are called physical, mental, or spiritual makes no difference.

It isn't enough to say that faith can do anything, because most people already believe this. What we have to do is not only realize that faith can do things, but we have to find out how faith is acquired, and then we have to use it for definite purposes. This is why we use meditation. These meditations are always affirmative statements, and they are always affirmative statements about something. In meditation, we try to arrive at certain definite conclusions that the mind accepts, and then we try to apply these conclusions to specific needs. Always, the meditation is for the purpose of causing the mind to accept something, to believe in something, and to expect something to happen.

To merely state that you believe God is all there is will not necessarily cause anything to happen. But when you believe that God is all there is, and when you have implicit confidence in the law of good, and when you use this belief for a definite purpose, then something will happen. The reason why it happens is that you are surrounded by a creative power, a creative mind, or a creative principle, whatever you choose to call it. You are surrounded by a creative power that actually does operate on your thinking. This is the key to the whole situation. Let us, then, learn to make known our requests with thanksgiving and in acceptance. Having done this, in that silent communion of our soul with its source, let us believe that the law of good will do the rest.

THE SELF YOU
OUGHT TO KNOW

One of our greatest needs is to come to know ourselves better. This is true of you and of me and of the whole human race, from those who lead the greatest nations to those with whom you rub elbows in the street.

As we think about the many problems that beset the world today, we are constantly searching for ways and means to effect a greater sense of security and to bring people a sense of peace and well being. We are grateful for the knowledge that science has revealed, but are reminded all too often that, in spite of the great advances in learning, most of us are at some time or another very conscious of a lack, a lack of an intangible something that could bring us an inner sense of sureness, an emotional poise, and harmony with other people.

Perhaps, in our seeking, we have looked too far abroad. One of the errors of our search for that which would satisfy our soul and make us whole has been that we have looked outside of ourselves, rather than within ourselves, for the answer to our needs. If each of us truly knew ourselves as what we really are, we could at once arrive at a place of dominion in our life where never again would we be subject to the turmoil of the world.

The two means by which we know ourselves are simple, but each must be followed. First, we come to know ourselves through the teachings of those who have devoted their lives to the study of the human being. We have come to know the nature and function of our physical being through those who have studied the human body. This has given us a knowledge of what the modern physician calls *soma*. *Soma* is a word that comes from the Greek and means the physical body.

With the advancement of the knowledge of the physical body, we have discovered that there is no point where the physical body can actually be separated from the mind. Even the individual cell, science tells us, is alive with intelligence. Since we have learned that there is intelligence in the body, this is the first way we come to understand ourselves.

The second way we come to understand ourselves is through the psyche. Now we see where modern physicians arrive at the term *psychosomatic*. They have joined to the Greek word *soma* the Greek term *psyche*, which means the mind. This has caused an entirely new concept of ourselves. We are coming to know that we are whole people only when we think of ourselves not only in terms of physical beings, but also in terms of mental beings.

A few years ago, your family doctor measured your pulse, listened to the beat of your heart, and wanted to see if there was a coating on your tongue. The doctor was studying the physical person only. Today, in the light of modern knowledge, doctors may still be concerned with the physical person, but beyond this they will almost certainly ask you, "What have you been thinking about? How have you been feeling about life and other people? What's on your mind?" They know now, better than anyone else, that if your body is to be healed, your emotions, your feelings, and your thoughts must also be healed, and this is why they ask you, "What's on your mind?"

This is not only true in the field of physical health; it is true in every branch of science. The physics teacher of twenty years ago handed students a piece of stone and told them to measure the density, the weight, and the size of it. Modern physicists take the same stone and look at it in an entirely different light. They aren't concerned as to how much it weighs, how dense it is, or what its size might be. They ask, "What invisible power can be released from this object?"

All knowledge is teaching us that the most important thing about anything or anyone is an invisible factor that you and I call the Spirit. It would be easy for us to so enshroud the Spirit with an element of mystery that it doesn't mean anything to us. But I believe we can and should arrive at a place where the spiritual self means something very definite to us.

Let us, then, consider one cell of the physical life, the kind of a cell that we find in the human body. This cell knows how to do everything that is necessary for it to do to be a perfect unit. In addition to knowing how to keep itself whole, it can also increase itself by division and become two cells. This is the way the body grows.

But here—and this is important—an organizing intelligence teaches these two cells how to work together in harmonious unity. As the number of cells increases, so does the organizing intelligence. We follow this increase until there are millions upon millions of cells constituting a very complex, a very beautiful, and a very wonderful human body. But how much more wonderful is the divine architect, or the organizing intelligence, that puts them together!

We have come to the place where we see the interrelation between mind and body. Science has verified the interrelationship of mind and body and has pointed to us the necessity of right thinking, as well as right feeling. But there is a third factor needed, and that is the spiritual one. No longer do we need to say, "I am a physical person alone." In the light of modern knowledge, we can say, "I am a spiritual person who uses a physical body." We can rightly say, "I am the intelligence that directs the cells of this body I use."

Let's look at this new understanding of the self in a practical light. One person may say, "I am sick and weary and defeated." By this very declaration, this person commands the cells of the body to carry out this negative expression. A person may say, "I can't," and the body responds. It has no choice but to respond, and the race is lost even before it even begins.

Jesus said, "I am the way, the truth, and the life...the Christ, the child of God." Jesus had found that for which we seek, the thing that alone can make us whole. He had come to know his spiritual self. He had identified himself with the spiritual architect. This was what gave him authority over life and brought him peace of mind, an inner security, and a love for all creation. If we are to rise above our limitations, would it not be well for us to follow in his steps? There have been many who have done this and who have found greater joy in living, greater health of body, and greater success.

When we say, "I am," there is a response to our decree, because in the very declaration about ourselves, it is not the limited person who speaks, but the universal mind. It is the infinite presence of good that speaks. When we say, "I am," we invoke the word of God, and God, the creator, speaks.

When we say, "I am," there is a law that responds to our thought. When we identify ourselves with good by saying, "I am complete and whole," the law of good has gone to work, and it will reflect good in our lives. When we say, "I am resentful" or "I am mad" or "I hate," the law responds to give form to what is in our mind, and this form is often what we know as illness and undesirable circumstances. How real this must have been to Job when he exclaimed, "The thing that I fear, I bring upon me."

When we realize that with every statement we make we are using a creative process, we will become careful of our thinking. We will be careful to stop creating the things we do not want. It has been said that fear is faith in the things we do not want. This is true because fear uses a creative process, and the creative law responds to give form to the thing feared. If the principle of cause and effect can work in one way, it can work with equal effect in another. So instead of exercising the power of fear, we should wake up to the importance of using the power of faith. Then we will be using the creative principle of mind to bring to us the things that are good.

No matter where we are or what our circumstance or condition in life is at this moment, we may begin to travel a new road. It is the divine heritage of every person to claim for themselves health and wholeness, and to expect, as a natural result, an inevitable consequence—the effect of wholeness—to follow.

When the way seems weary before you, stop for a moment and say, "I am not the lonely and saddened person that I seem to be. I, too, am the way, the life, and the truth. I, too, am a child of God." Let this declaration be as real to you as life itself. Feel it in the very depth of your heart, and expect the divine law to give form to this declaration quickly and easily and beautifully.

If your body has been expressing illness, change the authority that has permitted it to do so. Understand yourself. Know yourself to be the perfect life that is never ill but that is eternal wholeness itself. Say with an inner conviction, "I am the wholeness and the health of life, and I declare that my body expresses this wholeness in every cell of its structure."

Have the spiritual daring to launch out into life boldly, and declare for yourself, "I am wise with the wisdom of divine mind. I am strong in the strength of God." Remember that as you do this, you are using a creative principle, and the law must respond to the creative word that you speak.

199

We have decided that the physical body is made up of innumerable cells that must work together in complete harmony if physical health is to be maintained. We have decided that there is such a close relationship between our mind and our body that negative thoughts can disorganize the cell life in such a way as to produce sickness instead of health. We have also decided that when our mind comes into line with the divine architect who organized the body and created it and knows how to sustain it, we will have established the right psychosomatic relationship between body and mind, and we will enjoy better health.

We have concluded that our physical body is an organization of cells guided, directed, and sustained by divine intelligence. This is the real self. But we would have no self unless there were an infinite self. This makes each of us a cell in a universal body. Perhaps this is what is meant by the term *the body of God*, and just as there is a universal body, so is there also a universal intelligence that organizes and divinely directs the functions of this human body.

With this in mind, let's think of the whole human race as made up of innumerable human cells, all of which are put here by the same divine architect who created the individual cells in our personal physical bodies, and of course we know that this divine architect has made all races of one blood, because there is only one race, which is the human race, and only one God, who is the creator of us all.

Just as our thoughts of doubt, fear, and uncertainty, of insecurity and unhappiness can disorganize the functioning of our physical bodies, so universal thoughts of a like nature can disorganize all society and give wrong direction to everything we do, and just as bringing our thoughts into harmony with the divine architect and the spiritual plan that is perfect can produce this beneficial effect on the physical body, so the thoughts of all humanity, joined in one accord, can bring about a healing among the nations.

When we pray, we attune ourselves to the infinite intelligence that directs us in terms of love and goodwill. So clearly did Jesus understand this that at the moment of his greatest need, he said, "Lord, your will be done, and not mine." When we speak peace and when we speak wholeness and harmony, are we not also saying, "Lord, thy will be done," so that we, as individual cells, become harmonious parts of the body of the Creator? If our many voices would rise in common prayer to say again, "Your will be done," peace would come to humankind.

If, by a broad sweep, we could wave some mystical wand around the earth and re-identify all people as children of God, so that each, wherever they are, would say, "I am akin to the sovereign of peace. I am a harbinger of love and goodwill," certainly this invocation of the divine architect of the universe would call forth a response among all the nations that would melt in love every sword, that the plowshare should again turn the earth and bring forth a harvest of love and good for all.

YOU NEED NEVER GROW OLD

How old do you think you are? How old is old? When does a person get too old to enjoy life? Could it be possible that age is something that happens to our minds rather than to our bodies? Could a person be as young at eighty as they are at eighteen?

We have a woman lecturing for us who is eighty-three. You may possibly have seen her on the television program, *Life Begins at Eighty*. I know of no one who is keener of intellect or who has more spontaneous appreciation of life. Perhaps there is something to this theory that age is really in our minds. Surely, This Thing Called Life never grows old, and everything in nature seems to have something at the center of its being that perpetuates it.

We are told that every cell of the physical body is completely replaced every fourteen months. It seems funny to think that none of us is even a year-and-a-half old physically! Perhaps we have overlooked the meaning of This Thing Called Life as it functions in our physical bodies and haven't quite realized that it could keep us physically young indefinitely if we knew how to cooperate with it.

We are also told by one group of psychologists that there is no reason to suppose that our minds can grow old. They tell us that the mind is as young at ninety as it was at nine, that the only thing that is added to it is experience. Most psychologists agree that we learn less rapidly as years advance, but just as certainly and just as accurately. Some of the greatest scientific minds today are telling us that while time exists, age does not; that, in reality, time is not a way of measuring years and months and days, but rather time is a measurement of experience in a limitless life.

It does begin to look as though there is something wrong with the way we are putting things together in life. If it is true, in a broad sense, that neither the mind of itself nor the body of itself actually grows old, it is time for us to begin to ask what produces this aging process.

Suppose we think of mind in the same way we think about space. Space is everywhere. Many things exist in space. But space itself is never crowded, and it never gets old. No matter how much stuff you put into it, there is still just as much space. You can't wear it out. It never grows tired and it never becomes burdened with care.

Now let's introduce another thought, which is that God's mind is the only mind there is, and God is eternal, just as God's space is all the space there is and it also is eternal. We live because God is life, and we are able to think because the mind of God is in us. This is what Emerson meant when he said, "There is one mind common to all individuals."

Perhaps one of our troubles is that we have thought of ourselves as being separate from God, and in doing this, we have stored up a burden of care and worry in our minds. We also take on a feeling of responsibility that we aren't equipped to handle when we come to the place where we think, "I have a mind and you have a mind and someone else has a mind separate from God." If I am facing life and all its problems with my little mind, I feel inadequate to handle the situations that come along, because I am working all on my own, alone and without help from the power that is greater than I am.

What a load we will get off our minds when we learn that there is only one mind that carries every load. This is what Jesus meant when he said, "My yoke is easy and my burden is light."

Let's consider what wonderful miracles of life this one mind is always working in our bodies. When even one minute cell is injured or poisoned, there is an intelligence that immediately puts all of the chemistry of our body to work to replace it with a new cell that is whole, complete, and perfect. This is why wounds heal. This is what enables the little soldiers in our blood stream, which we call the corpuscles, to attack and defeat the enemy of disease.

It is almost startling how this intelligence works for us to give us health and comfort. Even in such a simple instance as stepping from a warm room into cold winter air, if we only had eyes to see it, we would witness a miracle of the one mind at work for our comfort. This one mind immediately causes the circulatory system, the respiratory system, and the digestive system all to go to work in such a way as to bring about an inner balance of temperature to counteract the cold wintry wind so as to keep the body free from pain and discomfort.

But nature doesn't seem to interfere with our thought processes in the same way, because we are individuals and have the right of self-choice, and so we are permitted to store up liabilities in the mind that tend to perpetuate our discomfort.

This one mind operates a wonderful factory in the human body. It has a furnace room to generate heat. It has a chemical plant to purify and dispose of poisons. It has a maintenance crew that keeps the machinery in good working order. It even has a lubricating system that keeps the joints oiled. There is the transportation system that carries supplies from one part of the factory to another and an interoffice communication system that would stagger the imagination of the greatest engineer.

This one mind, which of course is God, is capable of running the factory of this human body in perfect order. When Jesus said, "Consider the lilies," he could have been saying to us, "See how beautifully the factory is run when there is no interference with the natural and beautiful laws of God." It is self-evident that God's mind would be capable of running this factory of ours, which we call our bodies, if we would not throw wrenches of fear and doubt into the wheels of the machinery and if we would not overload the communication system and transportation system with the burdens of grief and worry and many other negative attitudes.

This is so simple that we stop and say to ourselves, "How is it and why is it that we ever arrived at a place where we stopped trusting the divine architect who created the factory and who is capable of operating it so perfectly?" If we could answer this question, we would know what is wrong with us.

The Bible says, "If there be one among a thousand to show uprightness, their flesh will be fresher than a child's; they will return to the days of their youth." We should not interpret this as meaning that we want to go back to childish ways, nor to former years, but that we do wish to keep the child always with us and not be burdened with the years that have passed. This is what repentance really means. It means to think another way. It means a new birth in the mind of the life that comes fresh, new, and perennial every moment of our existence. Every day is a fresh beginning. Every day is the world made new.

Nor does this mean that we have to recapture the physical body we possessed years ago, but rather that we must recognize the youth of the physical body that we have now, because there is not one cell in it that is over a year and a half old. Youth is in every muscle and in every fiber of our being. It is no wonder Jesus said, "The realm of God is like a child." So let's consider the mental attitudes of a child if we would recapture the dream we seem to have lost.

Then, we were young. We had so much to look forward to. The days were crowded with pleasure and happiness and fulfillment. We could hardly wait to get up the next morning to begin over again, because we had such an enthusiastic expectation. As a matter of fact, the first third of our life was spent in the enjoyment of the day in which we live, always with the anticipation of something more and bigger and better and brighter ahead. We were learning, we were studying, we were finding out how to do things, we were getting ready to live in a larger way. This is the period from the time we are born and became educated and knew that we had the security of our home and parents. We weren't afraid.

Now, we have reached maturity, and the world is still ahead of us. We fall in love, we get married and have children, and the cycle repeats itself. We live in them, and all the things that we have done for ourselves we now do for them, only in a multiplied way. This is what happens to the average person for the first half of life. People don't have time to grow old because they are busy with the pleasures of living, the enjoyment, the expectation, the enthusiasm, and the thought of the much and the more that is to come.

But too often, when these first two periods have passed, there isn't enough to look forward to. The kick has gone out of life. No one is happy who merely chases a mad ambition. We are really happy only in the creative things and in those things where we share the joys of living with others.

I am reminded of a story of a person whose life was marked by achievement. It was a typical American success story. This person made a vast fortune in the newspaper business and decided to retire. He went to one of the resort cities of Florida and became interested in dog racing. It became a hobby with him, and he bought the finest greyhound that money could buy. It was a beautiful animal.

One day, one of his friends met him and his dog slouching along sort of unenthusiastically on the boardwalk by the oceanfront, as though suddenly everything had gone stale with them. The friend said to him, "Why in the world aren't you out at the race track with this beautiful dog? One can tell by looking at it that it would be the finest dog on the tracks."

The newspaper man replied, "Well, it was the finest dog on the track, but now it's kind of like me. You see, last night he caught the rabbit."

There is a wonderful moral to this story. Neither this man nor his dog had learned that there are millions of uncaught rabbits. If we are going to have the youth of body and of mind, which is rightfully ours, we must always be looking for new goals to achieve, new ideas about which we can be enthused. We must keep our interest in life so active that there will be an element of wonder and surprise in simple, everyday things.

Life is activity, and when we stop being active, mentally or physically, we turn away from the newness of life itself, and those who grow old in years without an inward expectation and assurance that they are going to live forever will somewhere find the last part of their life overburdened with the thoughts of yesterday. Let's make up our minds that yesterday is forever gone. Tomorrow has not yet arrived. But today can be filled with wonder if we know that we stand always on the threshold of that which is wonderful and new.

I have never yet met one single individual who maintained this exuberant attitude in the last part of life unless they had faith, and I am talking about the kind of faith we all understand the meaning of—faith in something bigger than we are, in a power greater than we are, and a complete assurance that we are going to live forever, somewhere.

It's an interesting thing that, whether we know it or not, or whether we like it or not, our lives are so tied in to God, the living Spirit, that we cannot even remain young and enthusiastic unless we know that we are one with that which knows no age and with that which has no burdens.

I recently ran across this wonderful statement, taken from *The Sojourner*: "Nothing could be more pertinent or more stimulating, to those of us of advancing years, which reads: Youth is not a time of life—it is a state of mind."

Nobody grows old by merely living a number of years; people grow old only by deserting their ideals. Years wrinkle the skin, but to give up enthusiasm wrinkles the soul. Worry, doubt, self-distrust, fear, and despair—these are the long, long years that bow the head and turn the growing spirit back to dust.

Whether we are seventy or sixteen, there is in every being's heart the love of wonder, the sweet amazement at the stars and the star-like things and thoughts, the undaunted challenge of events, the unfailing childlike appetite for what next, and the joy in the game of life.

You are as young as your faith, as old as your doubt; as young as your self-confidence, as old as your fear; as young as your hope, as old as your despair.

The Miracle of
a Parent's Love

Mother's Day and Father's Day are the days when we celebrate the human love that symbolizes divine protection and tenderness. Just as we are cradled in the arms of a parent's love, so underneath us are also the everlasting arms, the great love of the universe from which we all spring.

It is wonderful that God has so provided for us that when we first enter this world, we come through the loving protection of our parent's care, and that there is waiting for every newborn babe the comfort, the warmth, and the tenderness of those whose hearts have been filled with an instinctive affection and a deep-seated desire to nurture and give to the miracle of life of which they have been a part.

This is the distinction between parental love and other forms of love. Parents impart their own being to their offspring, and we cannot doubt that, in a larger sense, it is God who imparts God's own being to all of us, making each of us an incarnation of the divine will, the divine life, and the divine love.

The home that is blessed with this assurance is indeed a happy one. The parents who realize the sacred trust imposed on them when they are given children to rear, and who have learned to trace the ancestry of their own children back to the divine parent, always have something to give their offspring that is lacking when this divine recognition is not there.

This gift of love is precious beyond rubies. It is the pearl of great price. If parents recognize this spiritual source of the love that they can give to their children, and if they impart this love to them, they will make a contribution to the mental, emotional, and physical health of future generations that science with all its achievement can never offer. Psychologists, with their technical knowledge, can explain the importance, indeed the necessity, because a child needs to have the emotional security of the parent's love, but only the parents are privileged to give it. No one else can do this for them.

How important, then, is parenthood. It is as though God had entrusted to parents the greatest gift of heaven to care for, to nurture, to love, to guide, until finally the infant passes into adulthood, and again the great drama of life is reenacted, thus keeping alive the great flow of the divine love that would nurture and care for all of us if we would let it.

Jesus said that he loved us because an infinite parent first loved him, and isn't it true that before we can feel the greater love, we must first feel loved by the universal parent of all life? We could not think unless there were first a universal thinker, nor could we live unless there were behind us a universal life, nor could we know the beauty and warmth of parental love unless there was, behind the scene of the human event, the universal parent—God—that imparts its own nature to each of its children.

Let us look into the process through which this divine givingness takes place. We have gotten used to thinking about the "fatherhood" of God. Jesus talked about "Our Father, which art in heaven," and very often when we pray, we begin our prayers with the words, "Dear Father." But must there not be, equal with the fatherhood of the infinite Spirit, also the motherhood? In the creative process of life, there is a blending of the two. There must be the Spirit that speaks the word of creation, and there must be the cosmic matrix that molds the divine idea into form and experience.

In watching this miracle of life and love, we see one of the most beautiful illustrations of the way God works. When the seed of life is burst into fruitfulness in human experience, the very spirit of parenthood inwardly prepares the expectant parent for the part they are to play in the creative process. The entire temperament is shifted in its balance, as though an invisible hand touched it and reshaped the physical and emotional processes.

There is born within the parent a desire and an interest and an expectation, which grow in their mind and heart even as the physical body of the child is taking form. Things they never thought of before come into their mind. They are equipped emotionally, so that it will not be a hardship for them to carry out the duties that are part of being a parent. They are being psychologically prepared by some cosmic teacher to become a nurse, a teacher, a counselor, and a spiritual comfort.

As we watch this process, we cannot help but recognize that the Divine Spirit knows how to take care of all our needs if we would let it. In a certain sense, life is all of us giving birth to new thoughts, new ideas, and new events, and why should we doubt that the same creative power that prepares the parent for the new baby will not also prepare us, physically and mentally, to give birth to new experiences? In a certain sense, the mind of everyone is a parent to the events and circumstances and conditions that take place in our life. In a very definite sense, the mind becomes impregnated with ideas, and in just as definite a sense the impregnated mind nurtures the idea into form.

We cannot doubt that the same intelligence provides the ways and methods and means through which every birth is to take place. Whether it is the physical birth of a baby or a new invention, everything comes from one source and through one creative process. Just as soon as the seed is hid in the ground, something stirs within it. As Lowell calls it, "an instinct within that reaches and towers and, groping blindly above it for light, climbs to a soul in grass and flowers." In just such a manner, our thoughts and hopes and ambitions, hid in the soil of faith and expectancy, will bear fruit after their own kind.

One of the things that has touched me more deeply than usual bears witness to the fact that hope hid in faith can bear the fruit of achievement.

I want to read to you a letter I recently received.

"Dear Dr. Holmes,

"With all my heart, I owe you this. One dreary, gray Sunday afternoon last autumn, I felt I had reached a new low in frustration, worry, and despair. My husband, insecure and anxious, had gone to the office to try to make up in time spent what he lacked in ability to produce. Lacking confidence, he had tried four times, after four years of college and twelve years of night study, to pass the state CPA examination. Some sense of failure, some deep feeling of insecurity, much of it based on his inability to pass the exam, had caught him in a vicious circle of defeat. I sat there idly, racking my brain for some idea, some way we could take, some method of helping him—switching on the radio, turning from station to station—when suddenly I heard, 'There is a power for good in this universe greater than us all.'

"I listened, comforted at first, relieved, and then suddenly exalted. The late afternoon sun seemed to break through the clouds, warming that October day and streamed into the room. A great feeling broke over me, not so much a realization of something new, but a recognition of something I had always known, which I had never quite called by its right name.

"From then on, I seemed to change, and I hoped that, if possible, I could find a way for myself, and that my husband might find his way also. I started going to your church, and when I could not go, I listened on Sunday afternoons. I began to know some of the richest happiness any person could know. Whenever my husband brought home problems, my tongue suddenly found some answers. I prayed that he would begin to feel what I was just beginning to experience. I found that just a word here and a word there seemed to stick in his mind (I could never just outrightly preach to him), and I began to see the burden lifting from his shoulders. Instead of taking the next examination, after several months of financial deprivement off work for study, he simply walked in with no preparation except what he had already accumulated over the years, and with a 'Well, what can I lose?' attitude, took the test. At work, I spent the day running back and forth from my desk to a quiet spot, praying.

"Tonight, Dr. Holmes, as I walked in the door of our home, my husband held out a trembling hand, and in it was a paper that said he had finally passed the State Board, and greater than it all, he told me that the first thing he did when he ripped it from the envelope was to 'thank God.'

"I cannot help but think of the help you must be to all young people like us—slaves to the age of the high I.Q. You tell us to seek and you will find, and you help us to find the right place in which to look."

Surely, this couple has experienced a new birth, and I have no doubt but that the divine intelligence that operated through this couple will continue to operate through them. It is even now preparing them to do their work intelligently and well, and everything that they need will come as an answer to their faith. Indeed, this is a new birth, and the child that is born from it will be whole and well, happy and prosperous.

Somehow or other, I love the thought that we are surrounded by the womb of nature that gives birth to all ideas, and who can doubt that the eternal Creator has already impregnated this womb with the invisible forms of everything necessary to the well being of humanity? This is what the apostle meant when he told us that we should think according to the pattern shown us on the Mount—the divine idea and ideal of our own child-ness with a power greater than we are, a love that broods over us and a will ready to fly through us into creative action.

Why should we doubt that we could use this creative principle to become the parent of health for our bodies? With our own minds, we can conceive of the perfection of God's life as wholeness for us, right here and right now. It is given to each of us to have an idea of health. We can have faith in this idea. We can expect it to come to life in our experience. We can believe that the divine process of creation provides everything necessary to give birth to this idea of health in our bodies. We can believe that even now it is reforming every atom and action and function of our being after its own divine pattern.

Any constructive idea we have can and will be acted on with the same intelligence, the same preparation for fulfillment, and the same dynamic power that gives birth to everything else in the universe.

Are we cradling our thoughts and ideas in the heart of love? Have we relaxed our minds and have we mentally and emotionally prepared ourselves to give birth to new experiences? Are we preparing for coming events with the same joyous enthusiasm with which the expectant parent prepares for the birth of the child? Did not the Bible tell us to make known our requests with thanksgiving and to believe with all our heart and soul and mind that that which we have accepted from the divine bounty will be given birth to in our experience, if we believe it will?

Let us, then, prepare our minds to give birth to a future bright with hope, constant with fulfillment, and in this preparation of the mind let's take thoughts similar to the following and meditate on them daily: "I live and move and have my being in the eternal presence of the parent-God. I know that this divine parent nurtures my every sincere prayer into fulfillment. There is nothing in my mind that fears or doubts that the creative principle of life will respond to that which I believe in my heart."

I like to use this statement in my own prayer: "I can do and be all things through God, the truth that strengthens me."

Spiritual Shock Absorbers

There was a time when we didn't have very good shock absorbers on our cars, and we bumped along the road, half the time clutching at the side of the car to keep from being thrown out.

This is a good illustration of our everyday life. Too much of the time we are startled or frightened or discouraged by the shocks we encounter. We bump along the road of life, sometimes up in the air and often clutching at the slightest straw to regain our poise and balance.

We can put the physical body into a car and float along on its shock absorbers, but what about this funny mind of ours, these strange and varied emotions we have? Have we found a shock absorber for the mind? Most of us haven't, and the road gets pretty rough at times. We are so busy trying to keep from falling out of the car that we often fail even to catch a glimpse of the beautiful landscape around us. Yes, we do need some kind of a mental shock absorber so that the disappointments of life and its fears and failures will not put us off balance.

Imagine that the mind is a vehicle we can liken to an automobile that carries us along on the varying pathways of life, either in comfort and enjoyment or dreading what's going to happen. The road ahead of us is always more or less uncertain, and life, if it is be happily lived, must be met with a good-natured flexibility, a calm, a poise, and a balance that enables us to go along with ourselves and others in peace and joy.

When we get up in the morning, if we have had a good night's sleep, we are reinvigorated by a silent process of nature that seems always to be rebuilding the worn out parts of the body. This is one of the great miracles of life. Wouldn't it be wonderful if we had an automobile that, when we put it in the garage for the night, would rebuild all of its parts while we were asleep? It would never wear out. And yet, this is exactly what nature is doing for our physical bodies.

But if we sleep fretfully and toss around during the night, dreaming of all sorts of confusing things, waking up and rolling over and going to sleep again, we don't feel very rested when morning comes. It is only when we let the bed hold us up that we relax. It is only when we have first gotten rid of our mental confusions that we can sleep well. It is only when we lie down in the soft arms of peace and relax our whole being that nature can restore our physical bodies.

Let go and really let God take over. Even this physical relaxation is impossible until the mind first relaxes, and so the mind also must be in repose. It must feel that it is resting in the arms of an infinite love and wisdom, that it is being guided and directed by an intelligence greater than its own and sustained by a power beyond its own. This we call faith, and it is the most necessary thing in life. Watch the miracle of nature when this takes place. Everything is made new during the night, and we arise like a new person, ready to meet another day with hope and anticipation and joy.

But now, we get into our mental automobiles and start out on our day's trip. Perhaps the coffee is cold, the eggs are too hard or too soft, the toast is burned, and perhaps we get so fussed up over these little things that we fail to meet our first hurdle, because we should enjoy our meals. But with every mouthful we swallow, we send a thought down inside of us that says, "This is bad." We could easily get indigestion from this. The food refuses to assimilate, and this affects the eliminative process, all because we failed to have the right mental attitude toward what we are doing.

Perhaps we begin the day by reading a lot of disconsolate news even while we are eating our breakfast. We haven't quite realized that there is something within us that can absorb all these petty shocks or these bumps in the road and kind of leap over them as though they weren't there. We go to the office or our place of business or occupation, whatever it may be, all upset. You know the rest of the story. We have all lived it over and over again, and I am afraid that in the process we often have become weary with the journey.

If science can build a physical absorber that takes up the shock when we drive our automobiles, why can't the mind build up a spiritual shock absorber that will absorb all the difficulties of the day with ease? An automobile isn't tired after it has completed its trip, and neither should we be weary with the day's work, which should be a thing of joy and not drudgery. Life should be a triumphant procession of the Spirit entering into every experience with joy and coming through every experience with victory.

Jesus, the wisest of the wise, said, "Come unto me all you that are weary and heavy laden, and I will give you rest. Take this yoke upon you and learn of me, because I am meek and lowly in spirit, and you will find rest unto your souls." Surely he must have discovered some spiritual shock absorber that you and I need to rediscover and apply to our everyday living. He gave us the key to this great discovery, this terrific recuperative power of the Spirit, when he told us, "Your Creator knows what you have need of," and when he said, "Take no anxious thought for tomorrow, but relax and let the invigorating power of the Spirit restore you continually."

The greatest single spiritual shock absorber is faith, confidence, trust, just a simple, childlike acceptance that life is made to live, just a letting go and letting God. But someone might say, "How can you suppose that God is interested in the little things I am doing?" I wonder if we have thought it over carefully enough. To God, the giver of all life, there is neither great nor small. The power that created the mountain and holds it in place also created the grain of sand, because one life has entered into everything. There is only one power behind all things and only one presence in all things. This is God, the living Spirit Almighty.

Children, who haven't learned of all the difficulties of life, sleep in peace and wake in joy and meet the new day with gladness. It is their day, and they are going to have fun living it. Nature provided children with spiritual shock absorbers when they were born, but they kind of mess them up as they get older, until finally they don't work at all, and the adult bumps along the pathway of life with fear and apprehension, hardly able to squeeze the slightest joy out of life. They tell us that when the mind looks forward to more pain from life than it does happiness, it begins to destroy the physical body.

You and I don't want to carry the proposition to this extent. We want to live and be happy. We want to be well and whole, and we want to get a kick out of life. Someone may say, "We are put here to learn all these lessons, and God is trying us out to see how much we can take." This is nonsense. It certainly has no relationship to the teaching of Jesus, who was always telling his followers about a peace and a joy that he had in life. Jesus was more filled with gladness than anyone else we know of, merely because he had spiritual shock absorbers that took up the stress and strain of life. He wasn't afraid of people or events. He wasn't afraid of losing his own life, and above and beyond everything else, he wasn't afraid of God. To him, life was made to live, just as a song is written to be sung and it really doesn't become a song until we sing it, and life doesn't become a thing of happiness until we live it happily.

We are all bound to meet with disappointments in life and with experiences that are unpleasant. The question is, how are we going to react to them? Have we something within us that absorbs their shocks and passes on to new endeavors? Is our faith greater than our fear? Do we have more certainty than doubt? Do we have a sense that we are living in a divine presence, or do we feel that we are isolated and alone?

There is one thing that can be said of all religions of the world, whether or not you and I agree with them. They have all taught that there is a power greater than we are. They have all been founded on the firm conviction that there is a love that can guide and an intelligence that will direct, if we let it. Every great religion has told us pretty much the same thing. Right now, today, when it is necessary for all of us to absorb a great many shocks nationally and internationally, everything else has failed. Our leaders everywhere are telling us that we ought to go back to church, and they are right. They are telling us that we ought to devote more time to spiritual things. They are one hundred percent right. We are on the verge of a great spiritual revival because of a terrific human need. The shock is more than we can absorb alone. The road is too hard without a guide, and the mind is distraught, unhappy, and forlorn without a faith.

Suppose you and I rebuild the automobile of the mind that we are riding in and see to it that we include spiritual shock absorbers, ones that will work under every situation. The process is simpler than it sounds, because we really do have control of our thinking and we really can think straight if we make up our minds to, and faith can be acquired if we practice using it.

First of all, we must have a deep conviction that God is right where we are—one all-sustaining power, one divine intelligence that knows everything, and one law of good that can govern all things if we let it, whether it be the little things in our everyday lives or the larger issues that arise in our communities, our country, or in the world. God governs all this, too. This is the first, the main, the fundamental proposition that we must start with.

Life has given us the power and the intelligence, but life refuses to live for us. This is because we are free. Life lets us alone to make the great discoveries for ourselves in order that we will finally come into the full stature of the children of God with complete liberty. And life knows what it is doing. It is shaping each one of us for an immortal destiny, an eternal pathway that will forever unfold. It has planted the seed of immortality within us and set us out on the pathway of self-experience in the greatest of all adventures: the discovery of the power hidden at the center of our own being, the power that is forever one with source, one with God.

We can train the mind to respond emotionally only to what we want it to respond to. We can train our minds to meet every issue with a sort of neutral attitude and then decide what experiences we wish to respond to. We now know that it is not the experience but our emotional reaction to it that will work for good or for ill.

We can train the mind to meet experiences, first of all with a neutral attitude, as though we say, "I have met up with a disappointment. So what? I refuse to become discouraged. I do not permit myself to be dismayed over anything. I push this particular thing out of my mind, and I know that out of it, something good will come." In this way, we mentally ward off the things that hurt us. We can train the mind to respond with emotion and feeling to that which is happy and constructive and life-giving, and we can say to these incidents, "I give you everything I have. I enter into you with joy and a great feeling of well being. I entertain you. I invite you."

We may meet with failure in something we wanted very much to do. But instead of reacting to it negatively, we can say, "That didn't work out, but it is going to. I have complete conviction that it will, somewhere along the line." So this shock is absorbed right down the road, in big things and in little, We can let that divine mechanism within us, which was put there for this purpose, absorb everything that doesn't belong to harmony and peace and happiness. We can, if we have an underlying faith in the all-sustaining power of the living Spirit.

This idea of spiritual shock absorbers is not an empty dream. There is something in us greater than anything we are ever going to meet, if we will only learn to relax mentally, to let go just like the rag doll we throw on the bed. Let us, in this sense, make rag dolls of ourselves and relax in every situation and let that wonderful power that is right where we are take up the shocks of life.

It all sounds so simple, doesn't it? Well, many a thing is simple that isn't easy. You and I know that it isn't always easy to think straight. It does require some effort. Of all the efforts we will ever make in life, this is the most worthwhile. It has been my opportunity and privilege to meet and talk with many thousands of people during my life, to know them intimately, to know of their thoughts and hopes, their longings and despairs, their fears and failures.

Among them, I have met those who have no spiritual shock absorbers, and they are a poor sight. Many have received the good news gladly, accepted it willingly, and practiced it consciously, and I have seen what has happened. The shocks really were absorbed, and they were made glad. Their hope rose to meet the sun of new experiences early in the fresh glow of a light that comes daily to the world and makes new the pathway of human experience.

Jesus understood about this light, and he often spoke of it. It is a light that lights everyone's path. I have met with those who refused to accept this light, not because they didn't want it or didn't feel the need of it, but merely because they couldn't quite come to believe in it. They were so filled with fear that they just couldn't quite accept that there is an all-sustaining power and presence into which they could relax.

You and I are convinced that there is such a light. We believe that there is a power greater than we are and a law of good right where we are, and above everything else, we are all learning to have a deeper faith and a higher conviction, just the simple, childlike faith that throws its little body into its parent's arms to be cradled to sleep in quiet contentment, just children playing on the shores of time in gladness.

This is our lost paradise that we must regain. It was lost only because we wandered away from it. It never has left us. The Bible tells us that underneath are the everlasting arms. Suppose we permit these arms to embrace us, to cradle us in loving care. Suppose we really relax and let go and let God. It is written that "they that dwell in the secret place of the Most High will abide under the shadow of the Almighty."

THE CONTAGIOUS
DISEASE OF ANXIETY

Recently, I read an article by a prominent psychiatrist telling us that anxiety is contagious. We are so familiar with the idea of contagious diseases that everyone accepts the fact without comment, but whoever heard of anxiety being contagious?

Whoever thought that children and dogs and cats and perhaps goldfish could be affected by the mental atmosphere of those around them? Well, they can be. It seems funny to think of a neurotic dog or a disconsolate goldfish. The world has come a long way in the last twenty-five years. Modern psychiatry is helping us to see how necessary it is that the atmosphere of the home be bright, cheerful, and happy. The home is the most important institution on earth.

Anxiety is contagious. Perhaps there is such a thing as a mental germ of fear that infects our minds, just as a physical germ infects the body. If so, this mental germ is a thing of thought. It is a mental and emotional attitude. It is a way of thinking.

We are told that we can acquire an anxiety complex by listening to those who are anxious. We are also told that people who are anxious should have someone to talk over their anxiety with, someone they can unload it on. Otherwise, the anxiety piles up in the mind until it finally becomes unendurable. Perhaps this is why the Bible tells us to confess our sins to one another, always, of course, remembering that the original meaning of the word *sin* is making a mistake, or missing the mark. And surely anxiety is a mistake, because it is missing the mark of happiness.

All anxiety is based on a feeling of insecurity. Jesus said that we should take no anxious thought for tomorrow, but live in such complete faith today that tomorrow will take care of itself. Perhaps if we were to follow the teaching of Jesus, we would be relieved of most of the strain of living. He knew a great deal more about these things than we do, and he told us of a friend in whom we may confide, who will share all our burdens and finally lift us out of unhappiness and fear.

Jesus called this friend "our Creator which art in heaven," not just your Creator and my Creator, but *our* Creator, everybody's Creator, the Creator of us all, the Spirit that is over all in all and through all and closer to us than our very breath. Didn't he say that God is in heaven, and heaven is right where you are, within and around you?

We all need a friend, one on whom we may rely, one who will always be there. We need a friend whose wisdom is great, in whom we may have implicit confidence, and one who will never let us down. This Thing Called Life had this all figured out long before you and I were born, and it implanted a spiritual self within each one of us—the real you. This friend is always with you, goes wherever you go, knows everything you think, and can answer your every need. It isn't necessary to be anxious at all. It isn't necessary to be afraid of anything.

Let's look at this proposition from another angle. If anxiety is contagious and can produce all kinds of unhappy results, why won't an opposite mental attitude produce an opposite result? In other words, faith alone can heal fear, just as love alone can erase hate.

But faith is more than just saying, "I am not afraid of anything." Faith is more than whistling in the dark to keep up your courage. Faith rises from a deep conviction that there is a power on which you may rely greater than you are—the power of This Thing Called Life. Faith is an assurance, both emotional and intellectual—that is, both of the mind and the heart—that God is right where you are, that good is available wherever you may be.

Faith is just as contagious as fear, and more so, because faith is built on a reality that is substantial and changeless and eternal, while fear is built on the belief that evil is equal to good. It would be as absurd as to believe that darkness is equal to light, because what happens to darkness when you bring in a light? It isn't there!

What happens to fear when you introduce faith? It no longer exists! What happens to your anxiety when confidence is restored? It disappears as a thief in the night. There is a place in your mind where thieves cannot break through and steal, where darkness cannot penetrate, where fear is unknown.

It is interesting to know that anxiety and fear are contagious. It is one of the best things that ever happened to us to have scientific evidence that this is so. But if we didn't go further than this, we would never discover a real healing. Any physician will tell you that a correct diagnosis of your case is essential to its healing. This is why so much time is spent in diagnosis in the modern medical clinics where people of science are devoting their lives to the well being of humanity. To find the cause of the trouble is the first intelligent step in knowing how to erase it. The same is true in modern psychiatry: finding the emotional reason behind a large portion of our physical ailments.

The physician is doing a wonderful job, and so is the psychiatrist. But we need something else. Just as we need a physician of the body, one who can determine the cause of our physical troubles, and a physician of the mind to find the seat of our emotional disturbances, so we also need a physician of the soul to find out why it is that we do not have a right relationship to This Thing Called Life. This is why Jesus is so often referred to as the great physician, because he introduced the idea of the availability of spiritual power.

It is well known that physical laws must be obeyed if one hopes to be physically well. It is also well known that mental and emotional laws must be adhered to, or we won't be mentally and emotionally balanced and poised. When it becomes equally known that spiritual laws also must be obeyed, we will have completed the cycle. We will have established a firm foundation for health, happiness, and success.

You can employ good physicians who will do everything in their power to help you physically. You can employ wise counselors who can help you to straighten out your emotional difficulties. But you cannot employ somebody to live for you. This is impossible. This is what is wonderful about This Thing Called Life. Its power is already implanted at the center of your being. Life has made the gift, but you will have to accept it. And you will have to use it.

If anxiety and fear are contagious, then so are unhappiness and doubt. They have mental germs of thought, too, that enter the mind and infect and stagnate and congest. Discouragement is contagious; hostility is contagious; animosity is contagious—each having its own germ of thought, each producing an effect like itself.

In medical science, physicians try to set up an immunity to disease. They inject serums in the body so it won't contract disease. And when people lack faith and confidence in life, they also have to have something injected in them that will make them immune to unhappiness and failure. For every doubt, they must find a faith that overpowers it.

This healing power is one with which you must become inoculated, so that when you enter an atmosphere of anxiety, you won't catch it; when you are surrounded by uncertain conditions, you will not lose confidence because the germ of fear has entered your thought. This healing power that will protect you is confidence in life itself. It is coming to know yourself, as the Bible says, "hid with Christ in God."

This is no mere figure of speech. It means exactly what it says and says exactly what it means. *Christ* means "Emmanuel," or God-with-you. To be hid with Christ in God means that you become aware of this divine thing within you, the presence that is in everything, the power that flows through everything, and the love and harmony that govern everything.

It is in this Spirit that you are to confide. It is with this Spirit that you are to commune. It must become more real to you than anything else in life—the supreme reality. The Spirit within you already, as Jesus said, knows what you have need of, knows how to plan your life with you. It is your friend who will never desert you. It is a power within you that knows nothing about weakness. It is a confidence within you that knows nothing about fear. And it is a warm, loving presence filled with light.

You may say, "How am I going to come to discover and know this wonderful thing within me? How am I going to make it real?" All you have to do is to act as though it were true. It isn't as though you had to learn some deep secret or discover some unknown river of life or concentrate some power or hold a lot of thoughts or develop a terrific will. It has nothing to do with any of this. All you have to do is to lay down your burdens and say, "Here I am, God." And in an instant, you will know that you are dealing with reality.

There isn't anywhere you go to find this power. You do not have to develop it. You didn't put the power there at all. It is already there; you merely use it. But you have to use it in confidence and trust.

There are a few simple rules that it would be wise for you to follow. First of all, if fear, anxiety, doubt, uncertainty, unhappiness, and discouragement are contagious, just don't think about them. Don't read about them and don't listen to them. If you find it necessary to be in their presence, just do what the Bible called "putting on the whole armor of faith." Nothing negative can penetrate this faith. When you put on the whole armor of faith, nothing can assail you.

Because faith is contagious, you will soon discover that people around you will begin to catch it. But this is a good germ. This is something we all want to become inoculated with. When you have a feeling of love, this too will be contagious, and you will be helping to dissipate any atmosphere of animosity around you.

What the world needs today, more than anything else and above all other things, is the actual proof, the real demonstration, the tangible result of an ever-growing number of people who are willing to try the greatest experiment in which the human mind can engage. Why don't you become a specialist in this field, first in your own life, next in your family, and next in all of your associations?

You have the power within yourself to change your own life, to have love and harmony around you, and to do your bit in helping the world. Surely this is a happy adventure. It is wonderful to discover a gold mine or an oil well, but here within you is the oil of the Spirit and the only real wealth there can be. Here in you is the wellspring of life, the eternal good, and the everlasting peace.

YOU GET WHAT YOU GIVE

We are all on the receiving line, wishing to get the most out of life. We wouldn't be normal if we didn't wish to enjoy living, because life is made to live. How could there be a song unless someone sings it?

But sometimes we fail to realize that there is an exact law of life telling us that, in the long run, we will only receive what we give. Suppose we had a lot of love in our hearts but refused to express it to those around us. We would soon become so bottled up with emotion that we would actually have a psychic, or mental and emotional, congestion.

Suppose we were filled with joy and had no way to express it. Our very joy might become a burden to us. Those who are filled with joy must lavish it on others. They must share it. In this way, they multiply their own happiness. Life has placed at the center of every person's being an urge to live, to love, to create, and to find fulfillment in joy, in happiness, and in communion with others.

Life is like a great force flowing through us, coming from a hidden source. It is the nature of a bird to soar and sing. It is the nature of a seed to burst with the gladness of its existence.

So it is with all the gifts of life that we possess. They, too, are here to be used. But too often we wait for some great day to arrive or some big event to transpire so that we may become heroic figures in the drama of life, and just as surely as we do this, we delay the day of our receiving because we have refused to give out such gifts as we already possess.

If we have only one talent, we should use it. In so doing, we will uncover other talents, and there is a talent we all possess, and that is the ability to be kind, to have an understanding heart and mind, to be tolerant and well-disposed toward others. In using this talent, we need not wait for any great event, because all around us there are those who are famished for just a little bit of human affection, just a morsel of kindness, just a bit of understanding, something that will make them feel that they, too, belong to life.

People respond to our sincere and friendly approach and meet us half way, giving back to us what we have first given to them. Try this out someday when you are walking down the street and see what happens. Just look into the eyes of the first dozen people you meet and, catching their eye, scowl at them. I venture to say that the majority of them will scowl back at you. Then the next dozen people you meet, smile at them, and I will be willing to bet that the majority of them will smile back at you.

Life really is a mirror reflecting back to each an exact likeness of our own image, and we are all mirrors reflecting back to others the attitudes that they reflect to us. But just as life is a mirror in human relationships, so it is also a mirror reflecting the mind of God back to us when we open up our consciousness in love and in adoration to the divine presence that surrounds everything and flows through everything.

This is the purpose of prayer and meditation, that we become so filled with the infinite wholeness that it reflects in everything we do. But it is necessary that we give it out to others. In this way, our own channels are kept clear, permitting the life greater than we are to flow through our mind into everything we touch, into what we say and do.

The passageway must be kept open at both ends, neither dammed up where we receive life nor blocked where it should be given out. Giving and receiving—this is the law of life. This is the way life is. Those who would receive all must give all, and those who give all will receive all.

Every act of human affection and love, of generous giving and receiving, of kindly relations with others, is an extension of the Spirit of life flowing through us. Life is the great giver, and each one of us a distributor. This was the first great teaching of Jesus, that we should recognize this divine presence in everything and in everyone and in ourselves.

The next great truth Jesus proclaimed was that there is a law of cause and effect that attracts to us those things we hold in consciousness. We will experience that which we have faith in. We will become like things we think about.

These are the two most important things in the teaching of Jesus: love and law. He taught them in every parable. He explained them over and over to his disciples. He proclaimed them in the Sermon on the Mount. He made it clear that life gives all, that we are supposed to receive this gift of heaven. But we cannot receive it for ourselves alone. The gifts of life can be multiplied only through our use of them, and so as we give, so will we receive; as we believe, so will it be done; as we think and expect, so will we experience.

The life and teaching of Jesus is an example of one who, having received all, gave everything away as fast as he got it. He used it, loosed it, and let it go, and because he did this, the loaves and fishes multiplied. Because he loved, the world has learned to love. Because he found God, countless millions have received comfort and hope and assurance.

Jesus discovered his oneness with God and, in so doing, discovered that all people are one with God. "The things that I do will you do also." He discovered the great power that always accompanies faith and conviction. It was his high mission to prove before the world that there is a power of good available to everyone, and it was equally a part of this great mission to show that, because we belong to God and are some part of life, we belong to each other.

In telling us that we should give, Jesus never implied that we should not receive. Rather, his inference was quite contrary to this, because his whole teaching was that we can give only as we have first received, but that it is only as we keep on giving that we will keep on receiving. Jesus did not teach that our giving should impoverish us, but rather that it should enrich us. He said we ought to enter into the joy of life. He said that we should be whole physically and mentally because we are first whole spiritually, and when he said that we should love our neighbors as ourselves, he did not say that we should hate ourselves because we love our neighbors. Rather, he meant exactly what he said—we should consider our neighbor equal to ourselves. As we give to them, we should also receive from them.

Let us, then, accept these few simple facts—simple, but as profound as life itself—because they contain the whole meaning of the teaching of the greatest, the wisest, and the most illumined person who ever lived. We have separated his teaching from the life we are living today. We have thought he was talking about a future state, when salvation would come because of our having suffered in this world. But this is far from the truth.

Jesus knew that God is everywhere. He knew that there is a perfection at the center of everything, a wholeness. He knew there is a spiritual law of good available here on earth.

Today, the world is as good as you make it or as evil as you think it. Today, you may meet as much love as you have to give. Today, you may enter into joy and happiness in yourself and with others, if you do not block its current through you. So we find Jesus telling us that we should make a daily practice of communing with God, and we should make it a daily practice to exercise our faith. He told us that when we do commune with God, we will receive inspiration from on high, and he said that when we use our faith, it will act exactly as a law of good, bringing to us those things we have faith in.

Then, he gave us, step by step, the way to do this. It was simple enough, so simple we have overlooked it. "Believe that you have, and you will receive. Give, and to you will be given. Love, and you will be loved." Daily, we should practice the divine presence, and this is done by affirming that the divine presence is here in us now. All that God has, all that God is, all that life can ever be, is here and now.

This is what we should affirm, and because this is true, we should affirm that the law of good goes before us and prepares the way, and we should expect good to happen. Knowing that there is no good to us alone, we should give and give, not until it hurts, but until, through the very act of living and giving, all hurt is taken out of life. We should give of faith until fear disappears. We should give of hope and confidence and expectation and acceptance until failure forevermore departs from us, and, seeing God in people and in things, we should so court this divine presence that to us it becomes the one solid and changeless reality, a rock in a weary land and a shelter in the time of storm.

You Will Live Forever

When the disciples of Jesus asked him, "What is God's relationship to the dead?" he answered, "God is not a God for the dead, but for the living, for all live unto God." Here is a plain and simple answer from the one who knew what he was talking about, the one who raised himself from the dead and showed himself to over to five hundred people afterwards. Here is a simple but sublime proof of the immortality and the on-going of the individual soul. Unto God, the great life, all are alive, because God is life.

The two great cornerstones of the Christian faith are the unique personality of every individual soul and the immortality of every person's life. Without these, the philosophy of Christianity would merely be a code of high ethics. It is this, and heaven, too.

Life is the gift of God. You and I didn't create it, nor can we destroy it. It is my personal conviction that everyone must finally arrive at a place of good. It is this hope and inward assurance that gives meaning to life and courage to endeavor.

But immortality should not be thought of as something that is going to take place. Rather, it should be thought of as something that now is taking place. We are Spirit now as much as we will or ever can become, and that spark within us, which I believe will continue after we have left this world, must finally be fanned into a divine blaze. Death is only the entrance to a larger life, a more complete fulfillment.

One of the greatest passages in the New Testament asks this question: "How are the dead raised up, and with what body do they come?" This question has been asked since time began. We are so used to thinking that what is real is only that which we can touch or taste or handle or weigh or measure. It is a little difficult to understand how there could be a spiritual body as well as a physical one. So Saint Paul answers his own question, "How is it the dead are raised up, and with what body do they come?" by saying, "There are also celestial bodies and bodies terrestrial. So also is the resurrection of the dead. It is sown in weakness; it is raised in power. It is sown a natural body; it is raised a spiritual body. There is a natural body (a physical body), and there is a spiritual body."

It is this spiritual body that St. Paul refers to that is immortal, and now, at long last, science is furnishing us with the proof of what we have always felt by some divine awareness within us. This Thing Called Life is not dependent on the physical body you and I are now using. In experiments conducted for the purpose of proving the transcendent powers of the mind, it has been demonstrated that even in this life it is possible to reproduce the activities of the physical senses without using the physical organs of these senses.

Life has already implanted within us the capacity to continue to live after this body is laid to rest. This is what the prophet meant when he said, "If ever the silver cord be loosed, then will the dust return to the earth as it was and the Spirit will return unto God who gave it." If you can prove that you can maintain all the activities and functions that are associated with your personality, and do this independently of the physical body, don't you think you would be going a long way toward proving that you are immortal now? You don't have to die to have eternal life. This is what is meant by that remarkable passage in the New Testament where it implies that those who come to believe in the truth of their being will not enter into death. They will become so aware of life that something will happen inside of them to make them know they are going to live forever.

Immortality is not something we purchase. It is the gift of life, and this gift is made to all people, not just to a few. You and I would be the most unhappy people on earth if we believed we were the only ones who were going to be immortal. There is something about life that demands a sharing of our living with others, and we couldn't possibly believe that the Divine enters into only a selected group of people. As St. Paul said, in the realm of God there is neither Jew nor Gentile, because God has made all people of one blood and stamped on each a divine individuality that is destined to exist forever, somewhere. How wonderful is this thought of the on-going of the human life. Well did the Apostle say, "O death, where is your sting? O grave, where is your victory?"

But the skeptic might ask, "How can you believe in something you have not seen?" Let us answer by asking another question. Do you believe in beauty? No artist ever saw beauty. It is something felt, and it is out of this feeling for beauty that the artist creates the object of art. All the biologists in the world have never seen life, and yet this is what they deal with. If you could put every psychologist on earth together, you would discover that psychology, which is the study of mental and emotional actions and reactions, has never seen the mind. Yet is there any sane person who doubts its existence? All the physicists on earth, who spend their whole time dealing with the primary energy, have never seen this energy, but they know it exists, and all the theologians crammed together have never seen the Spirit, and yet it is the Spirit that quickens.

Of course we haven't seen life, nor have we seen the principle of mathematics or of harmony. No one ever saw gravity, but we cannot doubt its existence. No, you have never seen the soul, the mind, the Spirit, or the vital force that energizes your physical body. You have never seen the hope and the faith and the inspiration that stimulates your mind to action. You have never seen that soft and enveloping presence that nestles as close to you as life itself. You have never seen God, the divine intelligence that holds everything in its grasp. But you have felt life, because you are it. It is here, or you wouldn't be alive.

The well known scientist Dr. Millikan has stated that we have as much evidence of the existence of the soul as we have of the atom. There is no doubt whatsoever in my own mind that all people are immortal, nor do I have any doubt that we have plenty of proof of this. But we are all human beings, and we do "long for the touch of a vanished hand or the sound of a voice that is stilled." Even in this longing, however, there is the hope and the assurance that those whom we have known and loved, and all others, still continue their individual pathways amid scenes as real as these.

This Thing Called Life has provided for everything necessary to our well being. When we entered this life, we were greeted with loving hands and tender hearts that gave us the care we needed until we were able to look after ourselves, and so it will be in the next life. Most of us have as many friends on the other side as we have here, and we know that "with the dawn, their happy faces smile, which we have loved long since and lost awhile."

Jesus said, "In my Creator's house are many mansions." Life is an eternal evolution, or unfoldment. When we are through with one experience, we enter another, always moving forward. Jesus did not say, "I am going to come back here again." Rather, he said, "I go to prepare a place for you there, that where I am, there you may be also."

Jesus plainly taught the progressive unfoldment of every individual soul, and this is the way we should think of our friends who have left this world—not as being less, but more themselves.

I sometimes wonder what our conduct would be if we all actually believed that we are immortal now, that we are living in the realm of God now, and that we are going to continue forever somewhere. I am not thinking of this as an idle dream or an empty theory, but rather in the light of a present reality. Wouldn't it give us more faith and confidence in life? Wouldn't it give us more courage and hope? Wouldn't we really have more human kindness and tolerance if we could see that everyone, including ourselves, is doing the best they can? Certainly we would live more enthusiastically if this were a complete conviction.

It is now known that when we look forward to more pain from life than pleasure, the mind begins to destroy the physical body. We cannot live enthusiastically and maintain the full vitality of youth unless there is the same expectancy in the mind that we had when we were young. The famous psychiatrist Dr. Carl Jung has said that the deep conviction of immortality is the best possible mental medicine, because where there is nothing to look forward to, there is no hope. Where there is no hope, there is no joy in living, and when there is no enthusiasm for life, the well-springs of our being begin to stagnate.

But to those who know that life goes on, every day is only another fresh beginning filled with hope and wonder. The thoughts of death pass completely from their consciousness. Age no longer hangs heavily over them, and the transition from this life to the next is looked forward to as a great adventure. I believe that the major part of physical illnesses that have been associated with age will eliminate themselves when we come to look forward to the larger life.

We should put all thought of fear or dread from our mind and live in joy and happiness, each day fulfilling the duties and entering into the joys of living, not as though we were either old or young, but from that broader basis that we are immortal souls now. As thoughts of age and uncertainty slip from the mind, there will come a new buoyancy in the step, a new lightness in the heart. This is the triumph of the Spirit. This is why Jesus said, on the eve of his departure, "Peace I leave with you, my peace I give unto you: not as the world gives give I unto you. Let not your heart be troubled, neither let it be afraid."

There is nothing to be afraid of in God's world, and God's world is the only world there is. There is nothing to die in God's life, and God's life is the only life there is. To understand this is our resurrection, because we are not to be resurrected from the dead; the real resurrection is from the belief that there are any dead.

It is the resurrected Christ we glorify today, as we lay a wreath of adoration before the cross of memory. For behold! the tomb is empty, the stone has been rolled away, and the radiant form of the child of God emerges clad in robes of light.

Your Invisible Guest

If God is all there is, it follows that the Spirit within us must be some part of the divine being. When we were born into this world, we were accompanied by a spiritual presence, which is the real self. But this spiritual self is pretty much an unknown guest to all of us. Yet we do feel its reality, because in moments of stress and strain, when the mind is distracted and the body exhausted, very often we find something new and strong and vibrant flowing into us, as though we were being recharged, remade, and revitalized by a power that seems outside us. And yet, this power really must be within.

Nothing is more important than that we should know ourselves. In search of this self-discovery, we naturally start with the physical body, and of course we believe in giving the body every chance to be well and healthy. We believe in proper diet and sane eating. We realize that we all need rest and relaxation. And certainly we accept the findings of modern medicine and surgery.

But nowadays we are told that it is difficult to tell just where the body leaves off and the mind begins. Many people are trying to discover just what the relationship between this elusive thing we call *mind* is to this other nearly as elusive a thing that we call *body.*

You and I certainly agree that we must have a happy mind if we wish to have a healthy body. But there is still another field that remains pretty much unknown, and that is the relationship of the Spirit within us to both the mind and the body. While we have bodies and while we have minds, we also are Spirit. And there is a Spirit within us that uses both mind and body, or as the Bible said, we are Spirit, soul, and body, which means Spirit, mind, and body. There can be no doubt but if we could bring these three ideas together in right arrangement, we would probably get over most of our troubles.

I believe that everyone, in a sense, has a guardian angel—the angel of our better self, the angel of the presence of God within us. There is at the very center of our mental and physical being such a divine presence, intimately personal to each one of us—the real self, which is forever one with God. Our whole endeavor, whether or not we know it, is to reach this real self and bring it into the mind. To become better acquainted with this inner Spirit should be one of the chief aims of life, because it is this Spirit within us that is the only direct avenue we have to God. The Bible calls this Spirit "Christ-in-us," the hope of glory, and it tells us that we should be transformed in our minds by putting off the old person and putting on the new one, which is Christ. It also says that God has given this inner Christ dominion over everything.

We all would like to have dominion over evil, over fear and doubt, over sickness and unhappiness. There is an intuition, an inner guide, at the center of every person's being, which, if we let it, can and will so direct our thoughts and acts that they will come into harmony with life. We all long to be made whole, and we all seek happiness. Everyone needs an inner tranquility and peace of mind, and everyone needs to feel that there is something about them that is as eternal as God. We can't help feeling this way. Nothing is more certain than that we didn't create ourselves and that, when we wake to self-consciousness, we already come face to face with an invisible guest—the incarnation of God in us, that thing which flows through us and animates us and gives us life and consciousness and intelligence.

Moreover, this divine presence within you and within me is a little different in each one of us. Life never reproduces itself. The resources of God are limitless. No things, people, or events are ever identical. Always, life seems to flow from an invisible source, and as it does this, it seems to create a different situation.

If this weren't true, life would be a continual monotony. And life is monotonous unless we find variations of self-expression. Some days, we want to sing and dance, and at other times, we wish to become quiet and meditative. At certain moments, we wish to pour out our whole soul in prayer and communion with the Spirit, and at other times, we have a desire to be active and express our feeling in creative living.

It has been completely demonstrated that when we block these avenues of self-expression and creative living, and inhibit their action through us, then we become emotionally congested. One of the interesting things about this is that when we do become emotionally congested, our intellects become confused. There is an unlived life at the center of everyone seeking expression, demanding attention.

I have no doubt that if we spent as much time becoming acquainted with this invisible guest, this Spirit within us, as we do denying its presence, we should discover a wholeness at the center of our being, a peace and a quiet contentment that would do away with all our confusions. I have no doubt but that if we were to completely surrender ourselves to this divine presence and let it guide us, everything would be all right in our lives.

But if each one of us is an individual in God and a person in our own right, then it is not going to be any use to pattern our lives after others. While it is necessary that we live together in peace, in harmony, and in cooperation, it certainly is never necessary that we imitate others. Probably this is the real spiritual secret of democracy, that countless numbers of people should learn how to live together while at the same time remaining themselves.

We find no difficulty over this in nature itself. The peach tree bears fruit beside the blooming rose, and the cactus on the desert has no controversy with the Joshua tree. Nor does the lofty mountain feel the need of lowering its peaks because it is surrounded by valleys. Nature is not confused, and if there is confusion in our lives, it is because we are not adhering to the laws of nature.

There are many things that you and I can do as individuals, an infinite variety of things. But one thing we should never overlook is that behind this variety, there is a unity, and within this unity, the creator of all has seen fit to place you and me as unique representations of itself. This also is a part of the democratic principle in that we never deny others their right to live and express themselves to the full, but each should and must reserve for themselves the divinity that makes them one with God and one with humankind, but at the same time has created each person a little different from all others. There is a place or a possibility in the life of every individual where, without interfering with anyone else, they may, can, and should expand to the fullness of the stature of a child of the living God.

It is wonderful to me—and indeed the most wonderful thought of all—to realize that there must be something at the center of my own being that is the gift of heaven, that makes me just a little different from everybody else, that says to me, "Follow such genius or ability as you have to the full. Don't be afraid of it. As long as it doesn't interfere with anyone else, it is right. As long as it is constructive, it is good. As long as it abides in love, it can harm no one."

I wonder how many of us take time to become acquainted with

this better self, this higher self, this inner self, this person of God whom you and I did not create but who seems to stand patiently waiting our recognition. If you were in business and found yourself confused, afraid, and perhaps defeated, and I were to say to you, "But there is something you have overlooked. You really have a silent partner. There really is an unknown guest, an invisible presence, a divine intelligence that knows how to do anything. There really is a guide that can take you by the hand and lead you down the pathway of the good life that leads to success and happiness," perhaps if I were to say this to you as you were on the verge of defeat, it might astound you. You could hardly believe that such a thing is possible.

But if you should become interested, you might ask, "How am I going to become acquainted with this great big something within me that you tell me knows no defeat, this divine intelligence that you say could guide or lead or direct me into right decisions and right acts that lead to success? How am I going to become acquainted with this inner presence that has no doubts, no apprehensions, no forebodings of evil?"

I might have to be very gentle with you, very kind, but I would have to be positive, because I wish to awaken within you the same faith that I have acquired. I want you to come to see something I have already felt. I want you to meet something within yourself that I know I have met within myself. Consequently, there would be no sense of criticism or condemnation because of the condition in which you find yourself. Rather, there would be a deep compassion, a great love for you, and a great desire to do everything in my power to place your physical and mental hand in the hand of that unerring guide that already is right where you are.

I have never yet met a person to whom I could not explain this, and I have never yet met a person who rejected the idea. When people tell me of the infidels and the agnostics and atheists and unbelievers,

I merely laugh inside, because I know there is no such person. I know that This Thing Called Life, which is God, makes such an imprint on all of us, whether or not we know it, that just the slightest turn of our thought will open up the mind to an influx of something greater.

I often say to such people who think that they don't believe in anything spiritual or higher than they are, "Why do you suppose it is that you can eat ham sandwiches and apple pie and baked potatoes, and have them turn into hair and fingernails and flesh and bone and blood? There already is a divine chemist within you who knows how to do all these things." I often say to such people, "What do you think it is that holds the planets in their places and sets the course of nature?" I often say, "The very gravitational force that holds you in place right where you sit or stand is a power greater than you are and contains an intelligence beyond yours."

Sometimes I say, "Don't you know that when you were born into this world and gradually acquired self-consciousness, you were merely responding to something inside you? And don't you know that when you shuffle off this mortal coil and your physical body is inert in death, that something must have left you, otherwise your body would still be running around?"

It is simple questions like these that startle people into the amazement of realizing that there is really more to people, as Walt Whitman said, than is contained between their hats and their bootstraps. There really is a Spirit in us, and this Spirit is always the one Spirit making itself known in a little different way. I have never yet met one single individual who refused to be guided to this real Spirit. I know this is quite a claim to make, but an experience of many years has taught me this simple fact, that all people believe in God and want to believe in themselves, and that the only trouble with any of us when we become confused and distraught is that we have slipped our mooring somewhere. We have disconnected the thread of intelligence that runs from the infinite to the finite, and in so doing, we really have missed the boat.

I have seen too many people reborn, remade, and renewed in mind and body, just through taking a little time to get acquainted with the better self, just through coming to recognize the invisible and almost unknown guest who accompanies everyone through life. Yes, I really do believe in the spiritual presence within, the angel of God's presence.

It seems to me one of the most wonderful concepts of life. What could be more amazing, more wonderful than the thought that, as isolated as I appear to be, as confused as we most certainly all are at times, there is still the invariable guide, there is still with us the divine intelligence that knows all the answers?

Those around us may desert us. The skeptic may laugh at such idealistic conceptions. And those who are so full of common sense that it oozes out of them may say, "You will have to show me." I am always reminded of that quiet inner assurance that needs no person outside itself to assure it, the divine presence that is positive and calm and sure.

It is no wonder that it has been written that the wisdom of humankind is foolishness to God. We have learned so much that isn't true. To you and to me, this means that perhaps we have to retrace our steps and start all over again. Just as we started as a babe in arms and gradually grew up to become adults, maybe we will have to start as another kind of babe in the arms of the Infinite and again grow up into a different kind of adulthood, into a new way or experiencing things because of a new vision.

There is no doubt but that the vision of the world has failed to reach its goal. It has blasted itself on the rocks of uncertainty and fear, and wrecked its life on the treacherous shores of unbelief. We need a chart and compass. We need a guide. We need a pilot. But not an external one, not someone else to tell us what to do or how we ought to do it or how to live, not someone else who wishes merely to impose their own will on ours. This is the pathway that leads to nowhere, where the trail runs out and stops. We need an inner guide. The miracle of it all is that we already have this guide. It has been there all the time, waiting for your acceptance.

So we should take time every day to form new habits of thought. We should take time, through meditation, to affirm the presence of the divine person, the whole person. This is something no one can do for us but ourselves. But those who will take the time, in sincerity and simplicity, to affirm the presence of divine intelligence guiding them, will soon discover that those moments spent in meditative prayer are always followed by a betterment in their circumstances and by a betterment in their physical body, as though some new life-giving force were being poured into it. Above everything else, they will find a peace and a sense of security without which no one can be happy or whole.

Yes, there is a divine presence at the center of your being. There is a Spirit in humankind, and to each one of us, it comes fresh and new and wonderful every day, and more wonderful as the days pass, the thing that you really are and that I really am, because God has willed it this way, the thing that is the gift of heaven and the decree of God.

It's Up to You

What do you think life holds in store for you? Do you look forward to success and happiness? Is yesterday a happy memory? And what about today? Did you ever think that the only yesterday you can live over again is in your own mind, and the only tomorrow you can live is also in your own mind? Your yesterdays, then, are merely memories, and your tomorrows anticipations. But just as today flows out of yesterday, so tomorrow will be the outcome of what you think today.

Are you, like all the rest of us, carrying a lot into today that you ought to let go of? If so, it's up to you to rearrange your thoughts about yesterday so that there won't be any fear or hurt carried over into today. It's up to you to look confidently forward to tomorrow, so that today you won't be plagued by the thoughts of what might happen in the future. There is no way to make today happy other than living as though today would be an endless succession of your heart's desire.

Did you ever take time out of your busy life to think things over and wonder what is behind This Thing Called Life? What is its purpose? Does it have a goal? Is there a meaning to it? Where do you fit into the whole scheme of things?

You, like everyone else, wish to be well, happy, and successful. Don't you think that This Thing Called Life must wish us all to have a full and glorious life? If this weren't true, why would you have all these secret longings of your heart? Your imagination must flow from some secret source. If this weren't true, how could new ideas be born in your mind? It seems as though there is an irresistible "something" trying to interpret itself through everything.

A little seed planted in the ground strives to express itself to blossom and bear fruit. The child happily plays with its blocks, and the adult dreams of more and better things. Since this feeling is in everything, everywhere, and at the very center of your being, you must be following a natural law of life when you conceive of greater possibilities, when you plan out new things to do, and when you wish with all the feeling that is in you to live more abundantly.

It is impossible to believe that life would have implanted this imagination and feeling at the center of your being unless it were possible of fulfillment. No matter how frustrated you and I may be, we surely cannot think that God is either frustrated or incomplete. We can only think of God as the giver of life.

Suppose someone were to tell you that life is what you make it, that it really is up to you, and that the imagination that paints all nature with such vivid colors is trying to do something for you—which of course it can only do *through* you—that will make your life warm and colorful.

Joseph Strauss, one of the world's greatest engineers, who built the Golden Gate Bridge, was a very dear friend of mine, and on many occasions I heard him say, "There isn't anything impossible if you have the will, the know-how, and the determination to make it come true, if you have the imagination to see it as a completed task and the feeling that all the forces of nature are behind you." He was a person of small physical stature, but he said to himself early in life, "I am going to live to build the biggest things that were ever built in the world." His dream came true because he knew that behind it there was the same power and intelligence that puts everything together.

Perhaps this accounts for the spiritual genius of Jesus, because he said, "It is not I but the Creator who dwells in me, the Creator does the works." He believed that it was his destiny to prove to the world that God is not far off, that life exists at the center of everything, waiting to be expressed, that hidden in the mind of all people is the spirit of God waiting to come forth, full-orbed, into self-expression.

Henry Ford believed that we are surrounded by divine ideas and impulses waiting to express themselves through us. Possibly you may say to yourself, "But I am not a spiritual genius. I am not a great scientist. I am just a little isolated piece of humanity with no particular opportunity to do something wonderful." How do you know that this is true? The great people of genius throughout the ages who have done things have all had great confidence in themselves. In some way that perhaps was largely unconscious to them, they have hooked up with the same intelligence and power that makes everything.

It isn't at all necessary that you and I become geniuses, but it certainly is right that we should live a full life, that we should be happy. It is right that we should be successful. It is right that we should spread joy and well being wherever we go. You and I know that this is the secret desire of everyone's life, and life would never have put that thought there unless it were true. God never lies to us.

Let us see if we cannot map out a little program, something direct and simple, and begin to act as though life is what we make it; begin to think and plan this way; begin to live and hope to this purpose. Where, then, and how will we begin?

If you were going to refurnish your house, perhaps you would start by going through each room and deciding what pieces of furniture you want to take out and what pieces you wish to leave in. You would form sort of a pattern of what you wish your home to look like when you get through, and you would work toward this end. You would move out everything undesirable and replace it with something you want to live with.

You would do this definitely and deliberately, and, having removed a certain piece of furniture, you wouldn't be dragging it back to clutter up the rooms. Rather, you would say, "I am done with that forever. I have something new and different to take its place, something that is comfortable to live with and beautiful." Gradually you would transform your home after the pattern of your desire.

You are really living in a mental house, and the furniture is thoughts and ideas. The house is decorated with the color of your own imagination. This particular home of yours no one can refurnish for you but yourself. So you will have to begin and carefully dispose of everything that isn't desirable. Remember, you are dealing with thoughts and ideas. You are dealing with hopes and aspirations. You are dealing with enthusiasm and vitality. When it comes down to the last analysis, you are really dealing with yourself.

Let us suppose that you are surrounded by a creative and intelligent law that always tends to bring into your experience those things that occupy your thought. In other words, let's deliberately imagine that thoughts are things and that the sum total of all your thinking decides what is going to happen to you. This is to be a new and a wonderful adventure in the art of living. It is going to call for faith, imagination, and the will to believe.

Would you be afraid to do this, that the very idea is too good to be true? Do you want some authority that will help to convince you that the idea is not too good to be true, that this is the way it is with life? There was never a great person who ever lived who did not follow this rule, whether they knew it or not, and the greatest one who ever lived definitely said that it is your Creator's good pleasure to give you the realm.

But what God has given, you will have to take. And this taking is an act of faith, and I think that it is an act of faith more through the imagination than it is through the will. Jesus never said anything about exercising willpower or concentration. Rather, he said you have to feel, to imagine. You have to actually believe. And when you do, there is a power that will respond to you as you believe. He said, "It is done unto you as you believe." He said to forgive yourself for the past, look forward to the future with calm and expectant confidence, and live today in the assurance that the divine Giver wishes to make the gift of life.

Coue said that when the will and the imagination are in conflict, the imagination invariably wins. In this philosophy, we are learning that we must identify ourselves with our desires if we hope for their fulfillment.

Go through your mental house, and see what thoughts you wish to remove. Don't be afraid to look at your unpleasant memories long enough to convince yourself that they need no longer be there. You can do this easily enough if you try. As you look at some unpleasant experience, just say to yourself, "It doesn't matter so much now. Perhaps I did the best I could, and if not, I am going to learn to do better. I am going to use that experience now as a stepping stone to something better. I certainly don't intend to drag it around with me."

You can loose all the burdens of yesterday if you have the will to do it. It's up to you. After having carefully gone over all previous experiences and straightened them out in your own imagination, forgive yourself and everybody else. Be sure there isn't anything in your memory that hurts you and nothing stored up there that resents anything.

This finally resolves itself into a calm and positive determination to drag out the old pieces of furniture you don't want and burn them up. They can't be there in your way if you burn them. Their ugly forms will be dissipated in the flame, and in this case, the flame will be your imagination, your feeling that every day starts fresh and new. Just as you no longer hold anything against anyone or anything, so life no longer will hold anything against you. We all remember too much that isn't pleasant. But nothing is more certain than that you can take out what you put in, and all the power of the universe is with you.

Having deliberately removed the obstructions of the past, it is up to you to view the future in the light of a new hope, in the fire and imagination of a new will, and in the quiet, positive determination of a greater faith. To all those things you have been anticipating that have an unpleasant odor to them, just deliberately say, "I am no longer going to think about these things. They don't belong to me." You will be in league with life when you do this.

Now you are really ready to refurnish your house, carefully choosing the things you will be contented to live with. Yes, there is a comfortable couch there by the window where the morning sun streams in. There is a chair there under the reading lamp. But be sure that you are not wasting your time reading about calamities or tragedies or sadness. This isn't going to do anyone any good. This would convert the couch into a bed of pain and the chair into a torture chamber.

This chair and couch and the morning sun streaming in and the restful shade of the evening lamp are only symbols of your inward thoughts and feelings about life. It is up to you to do this, and you can if you will. Remember, you are embarking on a new life. You are entering a new country. You are following a faith within you, implanted there by This Thing Called Life. You cannot fail.

Every night when you go to bed, say, "Today is done." Bless it and let it go. Say to yourself, "I rest in peace and wake in joy and live in the expectation of happiness." Every morning, bless the day in which you live. Give it the best you have. Live it with enthusiasm and joy. Yes, today is God's day. Make God's day your day, that all the days to come will be filled with light and all your hopes and aspirations find fulfillment.

Your Spiritual
Bank Account

We all know that we have to have money before we can spend it, and how comfortable it makes us feel to have a good fat checking account, an account big enough to draw on in emergencies without impoverishing us when it comes to paying for our ordinary needs.

But we have another kind of checking account which is equally important. I call it your spiritual bank account, because I believe there are great spiritual forces that we can draw on and deposit in our minds which can be used in an emergency, in any stress or strain of life.

Life has enough of everything and to spare. It contains love and faith and peace of mind and joy. Wouldn't it be wonderful if we could build up a spiritual bank account and hold it in reserve—an account that we know would be sufficient to meet any emergency in our lives? We are always being called on to meet emergencies—times when we need more love and tolerance, more kindness and understanding, a deeper faith and a higher hope. These are the real crises in our lives, and at such times, unless we have a vast amount of good stored up, we not only become impoverished but we sometimes become destitute of hope. And then despair takes the place of hope, and fear takes the place of faith. This is what we want to avoid.

How would it be if we all opened up a spiritual account with the Bank of Life itself, and, realizing that we are drawing on the Infinite, see to it that each day we are depositing enough hope and happiness and faith to more than meet any emergency that can possibly arise? The wonderful part about this proposition is that we know life contains all these things, and it wants to give them to us. It is intended by the divine scheme of things that we should have them. But how would we go about to open up such an account and be sure that we have enough of these qualities on deposit so that our checks will be honored whenever any emergency arises?

In our ordinary affairs, we know that we have to deposit money if we are going to draw checks on it. We know that the money is in a safe place and that the check will always be honored unless we overdraw the account. But in our ordinary affairs we have to earn the money. In a certain sense, this will be true of our spiritual bank account. But the earning of the supply or the substance for our spiritual bank account is a little different, because we earn the ability to draw on the bank of love only through having practiced love.

If God is love—and no sane person can doubt this—and if each one of us has, as we must have, immediate access to the love of God, then we earn the ability to draw on the Bank of Love in such degree as we first have practiced being lovable and kind.

We will earn the ability to draw on this bank through constant meditation and prayer and communion with the Infinite, using statements in our meditations similar to the following: "God is love, and all the love there is is mine now. I will endeavor to see something lovable in everyone I meet, in every situation I find myself in, and as I do this, I will accumulate a great storehouse to be deposited in my bank. Then, when some experience comes along which seems unkind or unlovable, I will be able to write a check on my Bank of Love, which will cover every liability of hate or of unkindness."

Here is one of the great secrets of nature: Those who have taken time to do this until they feel themselves to be in tune with love will find that when some incident arises in their experience that seems hateful or discordant, they can actually draw on a reserve force which they now have. They can actually apply this to the situation when it arises.

If you have accumulated a certain amount of love and then meet some situation where discord and strife seem to enter, you can just get quiet inside yourself and say, "I am bringing love to bear on this situation, a love that comprehends and includes everything, a love that has no hurt in it, a love that isn't afraid, a love that is calm and confident and sure of itself."

Right here is where what we call "the law of mind in action" comes into play. When you apply your thought of love directly to discordant situations and there is nothing in you that is afraid, your thought of love applied to that situation will heal it. If you have already deposited enough love in your own checking account, you will find that you can meet the situation, your check will be honored by the Bank of Life, and the situation that confronts you will be healed.

First of all, you have to have a firm conviction that God is love, and you must have an equally firm conviction that when you apply this principle of love to any problem, the very words you speak in your meditation or treatment or prayer will actually neutralize or overcome everything that opposes it.

This not an act of will. It has nothing to do with holding thoughts. It has nothing whatsoever to do with concentrating your mind or influencing people. It has to do only with this thought: God is love. God has already deposited love at the center of everyone's being, whether they know it or not, and this love that we now use is not only the greatest in the world, it is the supreme power. It is the perfect law, it is an actual fact, it is a reality.

Because you have deposited a love which can see around everything that contradicts it, and because you have ample love left in your own thought, you will find that the love you use, acting as law, will definitely overcome the fear and the hate and the sense of insecurity that come where there is a sense of lack of love.

Perfect love alone can cast out all fear. Love is always greater than fear. Fear is not really an enemy of love. All that fear can do is to cast a shadow across your pathway. But this shadow is dissipated when you look at it with love. You are not dealing with two opposing forces, but really you are dealing only with one force, which is absolute and positive and conclusive. But first you must have made the deposit with the Bank of Life.

Perhaps you have spent much time with yourself, straightening out all the little animosities you have and resolving them into the one great love, which is God. God never fails and love never fails, and you will never fail if you use the love that God is.

We have some other things that we want to deposit in the Bank of Life. Perhaps one of the most important is faith—faith in God, faith in yourself, faith in what you are doing, and faith in those around you. People without faith are so insecure, so shaken by circumstances, that they become unstable in everything. But we can draw on the greater reservoir of all faith which comes only through implicit, complete surrender of all our fears, whether they are big or little.

Faith is natural; fear is unnatural. Faith is positive; fear is negative. Faith is affirmative; fear is a denial of life. And we need a great deal of faith if we are going to meet all the fears and uncertainties that everyone encounters.

Just a little faith can't do this, just as you couldn't pay a thousand dollar debt with five hundred dollars. So it will be impossible to meet a trying circumstance unless you have a sufficient faith to cover all the fear. As a matter of fact, we have as much faith as we use. We have as much faith as we believe. And faith, too, acts like a law.

When Jesus stood before the tomb of Lazarus, he was confronted with the fear of death. He was confronted with the weeping and the wailing of the family. In a certain sense, he was also confronted with the whole human belief in death. You will remember that they told Jesus that he dare not roll the stone away from the tomb of Lazarus. The stone is a symbol of the obstruction that confronts us sometimes when we attempt to use our faith for definite purposes. How often we look at the stone. How often we think of the tomb with the dead inside. How seldom do we realize that God made that stone, and that what God put there, God can remove.

To put the proposition in another way, how seldom we realize that there are no obstructions to divine power. Perhaps, after all, the stone was only in our own mind. But Jesus lifted up his voice in communion with God. He raised his thought above the fear of the moment. I don't believe Jesus could have done this unless he had first spent much time drawing on the Bank of Life and depositing large amounts of faith to his own account.

On another occasion, he had said, "This kind comes out but by fasting and prayer," by communion with God. Jesus had spent much time alone with God until that which to us seems so unreal, so theoretical, was to him the one solid reality: God is life; God is power; and this power is available to us right now.

Jesus must have gradually accumulated a storehouse of faith, and when the emergency arose, he was able to stand calm and certain, uncaught by the fears or the weeping and wailing of others. He looked up, not down, and offered what seems in many ways to be the greatest short prayer of the ages: "Creator, I thank you that you hear me, that you hear me always." What sublime confidence! What infinite trust! What limitless assurance!

How many of us have enough faith deposited in the Bank of Life so that when fear confronts us we can boldly proclaim, without making any false claims, "My faith is sufficient. My trust is complete. My assurance is absolute. Creator, I thank you that you hear me. There is no doubt. There is no uncertainty, no hesitation"?

"And I know." What power and possibility is caught in these two simple words "I know." There is no question, there is no doubt. I know "that you hear me always." Not once in awhile. Not by and by. Not yesterday, but here today as I face this tomb. In the midst of all this doubt and fear and uncertainty, I know.

Carefully note what happened next. It is written that Jesus cried with a loud voice, "Lazarus, come forth!" Jesus could not have said "Lazarus, come forth!" with such assurance if he had been depending on his human willpower. He was merely standing still and watching the glory of life, with a calm assurance that his words were honored by a power greater than he—the power that we all have access to, life itself.

There are many other things that we must accumulate and deposit in the Bank of Life besides love and faith. Important among them is joy and happiness, because life has intended us to be glad. There is always a song when we know how to sing it and always a joy if we can find it. And, of course, we need to deposit a large amount of peace in our minds, a peace that rides above the storm of confusion and doubt and uncertainty that so often confronts us.

If you listen to peace, you will hear it, and somehow or other it will flood your whole being. Then, when you meet confusion, just write out your check on the Bank of Peace, and don't be afraid to sign it in the name of God. This is God's bank, and just as surely as you do this you will discover that your words of peace, acting as a law of good, will draw on a power greater than you are and liquidate the confusion.

What does this mean, other than practicing the presence of God, coming to know that you are in partnership with the original banker, the one who made the Bank of Life, but the one who, in a certain sense, must wait for us to join in this divine partnership?

There is a power that honors your faith. There is a love that meets love with love, a law that meets faith with faith and good with good—this law, this power, this divine presence that you and I never created. We had no more to do with it than we did with the creation of the wind or the stars. It was there before we ever recognized it, and it would be there even if we had no existence. But it doesn't seem to be there to you and to me until we believe in it and use it.

Let us then be certain that we open up our account with this great Bank of Life, because here and here alone is the real substance that we can draw on to purchase every good and beautiful thing that life has in store for us. Here alone is peace and joy and certainty. Here alone is freedom from fear and doubt. Let us then deliberately close all our accounts with the lesser banks, throw away the old checkbooks and forget them, and learn to turn daily to the one and only supreme source, which is God.

Make Your
Own Tomorrows

Life has set the stamp of individuality on your soul. You are different from any other person who ever lived. You are an individualized center in the consciousness of God. You are a personal activity in the action of God. You are you, and you are eternal, and you are free.

There is a power at the center of your being, a presence that knows neither lack, limitation, nor fear. This presence and power is at the center of all people and all things.

Let us suppose This Thing Called Life were to say to you, "All right, little one, from now on the game of life is entirely yours. Play it as you like. I am going to serve you, but don't fool yourself. I am going to reflect right back to you, and with exactness, what you really are. If you don't like what is happening, I am not going to be disturbed. You are the arbiter of your fate. You are the captain of your soul."

It is not always easy for us to control our thoughts. It is not easy in the midst of pain to think peace, in the midst of poverty to think abundance, in the midst of unhappiness to think joy. But if you do this, you will meet with success.

You are either attracting or repelling according to your mental attitudes. You are either identifying yourself with lack or with abundance, with love and friendship or with indifference. You cannot keep from attracting into your experience that which corresponds to the sum total of your thoughts. This law of attraction and repulsion works automatically. It is like the law of reflection. The reflection in a mirror corresponds to the image held before the mirror. Life is a mirror peopled with the forms of your own acceptance. Wherever a mental image is set up in it, an objective form will be created.

How careful, then, you should be to guard your thoughts, not only seeing to it that you keep them free from doubt and fear, accepting only the good, but equally you should consciously repel every thought that denies that good. Realizing that all action starts in and is a result of consciousness, prepare your mind to receive the best that life has to offer.

Realizing that you may, in your ignorance, have been using the power of your mind negatively (not because you were evil, but because of human ignorance, superstition, and fear, which to a certain degree permeate everyone's thought), you are not going to condemn yourself or anyone else because of this. If the light has come, the thing to do is to use it, forgetting the darkness. When the day of enlightenment dawns, the night of darkness disappears.

Stop blaming anyone or anything—people, circumstances, or situations—for what may be happening to you. This is futile. Your accumulated thought patterns are automatically re-sowing their own seeds in the creative medium of your mind. They will keep on doing this until you change them. Your hope lies in the fact that you can change these patterns.

This is not a process of merely making affirmations or holding thoughts. It is a process of the gradual re-education of your whole mental reaction to life.

Learn to convert thought patterns of sickness, unhappiness, fear, and doubt into patterns that conform to spiritual perfection. You cannot change a pattern of fear by maintaining an attitude of fear or by fluctuating between fear and faith. Make a picture of yourself as happy and successful. Since you are the only one who has complete access to your thought, you can do this for yourself better than anyone else can do it for you.

You have been told that all things are possible to those who believe. Accepting this as a principle of your being and analyzing it to its logical conclusion, you have come to understand that faith is not a nebulous something; it is an actual idea, a definite mental attitude, a positive acceptance.

Faith is most certainly a mental attitude. When a certain seeker came to Jesus and said, "Lord, I believe; help my unbelief," this person was only showing how human we all are, how human you are, how human everyone is. From the inspiration of this hope and the enthusiasm of the occasion, standing in the light of one whose wick of life was ever kept trimmed and burning, feeling the warmth and color of its eternal glow, the seeker exclaimed, "I believe!"

This was a simple, sincere, and enthusiastic response to the consciousness of one who had faith. But no sooner had this man exclaimed, "I believe" out of the enthusiasm of his will to believe, then old thought patterns arose to block his faith, and he said, "Help my unbelief."

This man was not a weak character. He was just a human being on the same quest in which all are engaged. He was only showing that faith is more than an objective statement, that perfect faith cannot exist while there are subjective contradictions that deny the affirmation of the lips.

It is only when the intellect is no longer obstructed by negative emotional reactions, arising out of the experiences of doubt and fear, that the word of the mouth can immediately bear fruit. There is nothing in this thought to be discouraged about, because the very fact that thoughts are things also carries with it this divine connotation that the thinker can change the thoughts, that we really are masters of our fate.

You are the thinker. You are the creator of thought patterns. You are the master of your fate. But you must exercise this mastership. Remember that thought patterns are acquired. Therefore, the mind that accepted them can reject them.

No doubt most of these patterns are unconsciously taken into the mind. This makes no difference at all. What is there you can consciously lose? Drop it out of your thought, refuse to think about it, refuse to feed it with the fire of imagination and feeling. Having nothing to live on, it will shrivel up and disappear. It is only the thought that is nourished that grows.

You are to believe with utmost simplicity and with complete faith that there is a pattern of your being, or a real spirit of you, that is as eternal as God, as indestructible as reality, and as changeless as truth. This pattern is seeking to manifest through you. Behind it is all the will and purpose of the universe, all the irresistible laws of being. Finally, it will win.

The greatest minds of the ages have accepted that such a pattern exists. Socrates called it his spirit; Jesus, his creator in heaven. Some ancient mystics called it Atman. Why don't you call it just *you*, your complete self? Surely this is what they all have meant.

You already know that you live. You know that your life is peopled with events, persons coming and going, happenings that take place in your everyday experience, the thoughts in your own mind, the activities of your own affairs, the circulation of blood in your body. You already understand the presence of life.

It is this life in you, as you, that is the true actor in everything you do, but since you are an individual, even the Spirit cannot make the gift of life unless you accept it. Life may have given everything to you, but only that which you accept is yours to use. Life makes things out of itself through the simple and direct process of itself becoming that which it makes. This is why it is written that the word of power, of life and action is in your own mouth—in your thought.

This Thing Called Life works for you through your belief. All things are possible to This Thing Called Life; therefore, everything is possible to you in such degree as you can believe in and accept the operation of the Spirit in your life. Learn to become consciously aware of the divine presence and the divine power, the wholeness of truth, of love, of reason, and of a sound mind. Instead of dwelling on negative thoughts, cause your mind to dwell on peace and joy. Know that the power of the invisible Spirit is working in and through you now, at this very moment. Lay hold of this realization with complete certainty.

Often you may find that even though you start with an enthusiastic conviction, you become stranded on the rocks of unbelief. Refuse to let this discourage you. The law continues to be that it is done unto you as you believe. No matter how subtle the thoughts of lack, fear, uncertainty, or loneliness may be, they do not belong to you. Your affirmation can erase them.

No matter what the negations of yesterday may have been, your affirmations of today may rise triumphant over them. This is the highest hope ever placed before the vision of your search for something that can make you whole. The evil of all your yesterdays can vanish into nothingness. If you can see beauty instead of ugliness, beauty will appear. Cease weeping over the mistakes of yesterday, and, steadfastly beholding the face of the great and divine reality, walk in that light where there is no darkness.

Become master of your thinking, and thus master of your fate. There is no law of human heredity imposed on you. Evil has no history.

Limitation has no past. That which is opposed to good has no future. The eternal now is forever filled with the presence of perfect life. You always have been and forever will remain a complete and perfect expression of the eternal mind, which is God, the living Spirit Almighty.

ERNEST SHURTLEFF HOLMES (1887–1960), an ordained Divine Science minister, was founder of a spiritual movement known as Religious Science, a part of the New Thought movement, whose spiritual philosophy is known as Science of Mind. He was the author of *The Science of Mind* and numerous other metaphysical books, as well as founder of *Science of Mind* magazine, a monthly in continuous publication since 1927.

NEWT LIST is the foremost publisher of updated editions of spiritual classic texts. Newt List titles are edited to provide contemporary language structure and idioms that have evolved since the original manuscript was published. We revise punctuation and capitalizations, and adjust sentence structure when appropriate, as well as update certain words or terms that have since become obscure, as long as those changes do not affect the author's intention or meaning. More valuable for readers today, though, is Newt List's procedure of adjusting gender forms. In the time of original publication, these classic books generally used masculine forms when referring to God or humankind. Newt List updates all its titles using gender-neutral language, making the ideas in them apply more broadly to all readers.

newt
LIST

For more books by Ernest Holmes
and other New Thought authors,
visit NewtList.com.

Also from Newt List!

"How to" lessons on
relevant topics.

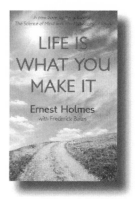

Ideas and techniques
for changing your life.

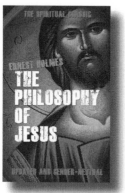

Understanding the life
and example of Jesus.

Interactive meditations
for greater mindfulness.

www.NewtList.com

Made in the USA
Columbia, SC
18 May 2019